D0411271

GOOD HOUSEKEEPING
Small Space
Gardening

By the same author

HOW TO CHEAT AT GARDENING

GOOD HOUSEKEEPING
Small Space Gardening

Hazel Evans

Illustrations by Chris Evans

STIRLING
DISTRICT
LIBRARY

EBURY PRESS
LONDON

First published in Great Britain in 1974 by
Ebury Press, 276 Vauxhall Bridge Road, London SW1 v 1HF
Second impression 1975

© Hazel Evans 1974

All rights reserved. No part of this publication may
be recorded, stored in a retrieval system, or transmitted,
in any form or by any means, electronic, mechanical,
photocopying, recording or otherwise, without the prior
permission of the copyright owner.

ISBN 0 85223 053 2

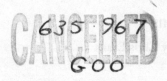
CANCELLED
635.967
GOO

Printed in Great Britain by
Ebenezer Baylis & Son Ltd
The Trinity Press, Worcester, and London
and bound by
Redwood Burn Ltd
Royal Mills, Esher, Surrey

To my mother

To my mother

Contents

Contents

1 The Sky's the Limit

WHEN WE first moved from a huge Victorian house in Surrey with an acre of ground, to a cottage in Sussex with no garden at all, really, just a tiny courtyard with walls 20 ft. high, a fashion designer friend took one look at the yard and said 'There's only one thing you can do with *that* – keep gorillas in it'.

It looked as if it would get no sun at all, and at times I felt like taking his advice, and that of the lady at the bicycle shop round the corner who said that she'd thought of buying the house but decided not to because she couldn't bear looking out of a kitchen window on to *that* wall, and shouldn't I put up lace curtains? But I found in fact that this kind of gardening was a new challenge, a real opportunity to have a go at a totally different kind of cultivating; it became a matter of pride with me to see just how much in the way of foliage and flowers I could conjure up out of the space. I grew things in everything from old baked bean cans to an oil drum, I was out every night in spring sowing annuals. In doing all this I've learned a lot about 'no-garden gardening', and made a lot of friends among people with similar plots and problems.

Do something spectacular
The motto is never give up, even if all you've got is a balcony or a window box or two. The more unpromising your surroundings are, the more you must be spurred on to do something spectacular. Now with trellis on the walls, a fake mirrored doorway and the outside loo demolished with a small pond and fountain installed instead (there was running water laid on, naturally!) it is really beginning to look like something. I kept the Victorian cistern up on the wall, painted it white and have begonias growing in it but I have discarded the chain. You couldn't imagine anything further from a gorilla pit, I can sit out of an evening (yes, it *does* get sun in summer

A*

Begonias growing in a Victorian cistern

though part of it faces north) on my white wrought iron chairs and admire my newly planted deep purple clematis, The President, scrambling up the wall. I didn't buy it until May but it rewarded me with some flowers this year, all the same. And showering down to meet it from the thicket on the hill above, is the wild clematis, old man's beard, with its little white flowers.

I've conjured up no end of new space for window boxes that sit happily on the cottage's broad window sills and which are filled at the moment with a mixture of geraniums, bedding begonias and dwarf tomato plants to give a technicolour display. Even the window box in the bathroom has a fine crop of nasturtiums, sweet peas and tomatoes again which, although they face east, have progressed more than anywhere else. The Russian vine, *Polygonum baldschuanicum*, which I dug up from our Surrey garden, has roared ahead round the side of the house, making about 20 ft of growth and festoons of flowers, disguising a bald brick wall and making a curtain of creepers over a rather plain window in it. (A word of warning about this useful but very vigorous plant; if you let it, it can take over in a small garden but it has its uses if you need a quick-growing cover or screen.) The miniscule ribbon of soil in the front of the house was raised and filled with roses, again transplanted from our old garden and we are, as usual, making wine from the heavily scented petals. Three grape vines – two Seyve-Villards and one Madeleine Angevine are laden with bunches of luscious grapes – they're in their third year now and although they, too, were transplanted they have produced lots of fruit and are obligingly climbing their way up the front of the house.

In front of the dustbins and a heap of builder's gravel waiting to be used for further work, I have placed some Versailles tubs, white-painted, with runner beans trained up bamboos and plenty of flowers and pods, while among them the dwarf peas gave a reasonable crop too. I conjured up a narrow bed along the south side of the house, making sure it wouldn't be in the way of cars backing in, by simply laying bricks, two courses high, one brick wide, with a space about a window box's width from the wall. I filled it with soil taken from our vineyard up the road and planted it with tomatoes and sunflowers and a marrow plant that I purchased on impulse and which is now threatening to march out into the street.

Herbs on the sill

In boxes in front of our dining room windows I've had great success with dill, coriander for Tandoori cooking and curries, sage (which I shall now move to a larger bed) and marjoram which I found growing wild in a field – after much attention in the way of watering, it has established itself well, has a more pungent scent for pâtés than the bought versions of the herb, and is threatening a take-over of the whole window box. Rue grows well here too; it's rather an odd-man-out in the herb family and is little used in cooking but I like it snipped over a salad. I've had disappointments, though, over chives and fennel but I shall try again next year, somewhere else.

On the kitchen window sill itself I have herbs again, growing in empty tins which have been given a coat of green enamel. I have several different varieties of mint, kept well under control – spearmint, peppermint and pennyroyal, some caraway too, for its seeds, and of course a few cloves of garlic. We've a curious split-level piece of garden up high (we live on the side of a hill), a tiny patch only a few feet square, but I've planted a wisteria in the corner and it is already coming down the wall as I want it to, thriving in the chalky soil. I've learned to use tubs, tins, anything – rather the way the Mediterranean peoples do – on the side of steps, on narrow sills, hung from the eaves of a roof. In them I grow other things, but mainly the good-tempered geranium, which doesn't need as much watering as most, and the nasturtium which gives such a wonderful display of colour for so little cost; it brightens up herb boxes which might otherwise appear to be all green (though the dill gives a splendid display of feathery leaves that look like maidenhair fern).

Next year I shall go on pinching extra flower beds along the sides of walls and plant a climber in a pot to shade our front porch. Another thing I shall do is plant some fruit trees, espalier fashion, for decoration as well as use. Apples, plums, pears and both sweet and morello cherries will grow beautifully against a wall, while the peach, the quince and the medlar are a good choice too. I shall also transplant our fig from Surrey and put it in a sunny bed. Two spectacular successes are the rhododendrons which I once had on an acid soil, which hated the clay-like earth they were forced to live in in our part of Surrey and which are now positively flourishing in Sussex. One is growing in a specially-made bed of acid soil, pinched from my sister, and in a corner of our courtyard another is growing in a chalky soil in a concrete tub, but has changed from a sickly yellow

A split-level garden, with wisteria growing down

colour to a gorgeous deep green – and flowered too – after being fed with copious amounts of iron in the form of Sequestrene.

The snag that I've found from container and window box gardening is that you are forever out with a watering can, especially in a hot dry summer, but it is by far outweighed by the advantages:

13

little or no weeding, no digging either, and with the individual treatment that they are bound to get as you potter from one pot to another, the plants reward you with better growth, more colour and more fruit. You can break a lot of rules too – there is nothing yet that I have found is impossible to grow, given a large enough container, and I'm especially proud of my herbs and vegetables, conjured up from almost nothing. Potatoes, too, will grow splendidly under black polythene in tubs and in narrow beds – and when I think of all the time I have wasted in the past, earthing them up and groping for them in the soil, I realise how lucky I am to have discovered this simple way of getting a supply, however small, each year.

The most unusual things come to your aid when you're coping with a very small garden – a patio or balcony for instance can be easily heated by electricity or even by gas. In fact you can eat out by gaslight now with the aid of several interesting-looking lamps – one like an ordinary gas mantle and another like a conventional Victorian street lamp. If you like barbecues you can buy a gas-fired one which is free-standing (it works from a gas cylinder) and which heats 'coals' made from pumice stone which cook your meat and sausages with that authentic barbecue smoky flavour; apparently what makes it taste like that is the fat dripping off the food on to the fire and then making smoke.

A screen of living plants

There's really no limit to what you can do with small space gardening, even if you are simply stuck with a flat – something more and more people are choosing as a mode of life either by choice or by compulsion. In a flat quite often all you normally see is a wilderness of concrete when you look out of the window, so if you are in any way a garden lover then you must create your own screen of living plants. But gardening in a flat can cause several problems; the containers used indoors must have removable trays or be designed so you can water them without making a mess on the floor. A balcony may offer all sorts of opportunities in the way of exotic, almost sub-tropical plants, but you must be sure that when you water them you are not sprinkling the people down below as well. Remember that in a flat or on a balcony you are almost certainly getting all your light from one direction, so it is important to 'turn' your plants occasionally, if you want to avoid their becoming one-sided in growth. Another thing to bear in mind is that light-weight containers are best, for not only will you have to hump them around from time to time, full of damp soil, but some balconies and most roof gardens have a limit to the weight they can take and it is obviously lunatic to exceed that.

Talking to your flowers

Recent research indicates the possibility that plants are affected by other factors than light and water. A series of experiments in which a man registered great distress and a house plant on the window sill beside him behaved in the same way, are now making the scientists wonder if perhaps plants *do* respond to outside impulses. Indeed the Russians who could normally be called prosaic about these things are conducting experiments at this moment in talking to plants to make them grow, so I'm beginning to take it seriously. I went to interview a religious community in the north of Scotland who had coaxed a fantastic garden out of the most unrewarding soil – nothing more than sandy dust. They told me that they talked to their plants to encourage growth. I was sceptical at the time, but since then I have had reason to wonder, having bought a job lot of bulbs through a magazine offer, some of which I did not particularly like. When the time came for planting, when I had to put in the bulbs I was not at all keen on, I found that I was muttering and swearing to myself at having to do the job in hand – and not one of them has come up. All the rest have flourished, but this particular batch, only part of the order, have stubbornly refused to grow.

Remember if you are planting flowers in a flat not only to group them together for company – there is no doubt that plants grow better together – but to concentrate on fragrance, too, if they are going to grow on a window sill. Night-scented stocks are easy and worthwhile to grow in a window box; despite their rather gangling appearance, they perfume the city air in a wonderful way. The miniature orange, *Citrus mitis*, has a strong perfume and if you are lucky you will get fruit from it, while in early spring you can't beat hyacinths for scented flowers. Remember that with the use of a fluorescent tube (40 watt ones are quite adequate), you can not only light your plants at night but also give them extra growing time – this is particularly valuable in the case of plants like African violets. Some of the scented leaf geraniums (*Pelargoniums*) will perfume a room, especially if it is centrally heated.

Gardens in bottles and tanks

Don't forget, too, if you are short of time, that a bottle garden is good sense in a small flat; once properly planted, it can more or less be left to look after itself. A bottle garden doesn't need a sunny sill, either, for too much warmth will tend to exhaust its contents. You usually see gardens planted this way in large carboys, but more fun in my opinion are the much smaller ones planted in a dimpled bottle that is stood on its side – the kind of bottle you might find a miniature ship in. Alternatively you could use a discarded aquarium for the job. The plants in a bottle or aquarium need little or no watering; what evaporates runs back down the glass and into the soil. So this makes an ideal basic garden for the busy person with a small flat who is away quite a lot – in fact it's the best basic indoor garden to start with if you are not used to house plants.

You're quite safe growing anything that likes a humid atmosphere in a bottle – ferns or orchids for instance, ivy which likes plenty of damp and even tiny seedling trees which practically bonsai themselves grown this way. Filling your bottle ready to receive its plants is easy – you carefully shake in, through a home-made paper funnel, some pieces of charcoal first, or tiny pebbles, then some leaf-mould, vermiculite or sphagnum moss to make a soft bed. This is a relatively easy thing to do if your bottle is being stood upright. If it is to go on its side, then the easiest way to put the charcoal and soil in is to rig up a special gadget – a teaspoon or dessertspoon wired on to a piece of stick which will go through the neck of the bottle. Lay the bottle on its side and shovel first the charcoal and then the growing medium in. You can use the other end of the stick to make a hole for each of the plants.

Lower each plant in on a piece of wire, then use a long, stiff artist's brush or something similar to cover the roots with the soil.

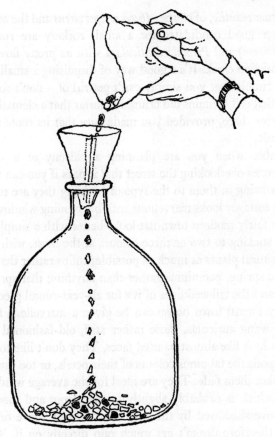

Preparing the base for a bottle garden

Finally water the contents with an atomiser or fine mist spray, plug with cotton wool, and you've finished. For really cramped space you could even use a large balloon brandy glass to grow a miniature plant in, provided you covered the top with a sheet of glass.

Making a garden in miniature

Talking of miniatures, there is such a lot you can do with them in a very small garden. Sometimes a tiny flower bed against a wall would look best converted into a rockery and covered with alpines. The edelweiss (*Leontopodium*) will grow happily this way and so

17

will *Alyssum saxatile*, of course, *Iberis sempervirens* and the aubretias. Two other good candidates for a small rockery are rock roses (*Helianthemum*) and *Primula denticulata* with its pretty flower head like a dandelion clock. It's a good way of disguising a small heap of builder's rubble that you simply can't get rid of – don't forget, by the way, that if it contains old crumbly mortar that a clematis would love to grow there, provided you made sure that its roots are kept in the shade.

Remember when you are planning a balcony or a series of window boxes overlooking the street that it pays if you can to relate what is growing in them to the type of building they are to adorn. Anything cottagey looks marvellous with burgeoning window boxes, whereas a fairly modern town flat looks better with a simple planting plan, sticking to two or three colours at the most, with the use of architectural plants as much as possible; tulips rather than daffodils in the spring, geraniums rather than anything that sprawls, in summer, and the tailored lines of ivy for all-year-round greenery.

A really formal town house can be given a marvellous frontage of colour using auriculas, those rather stiff, old-fashioned flowers with what look like almost painted faces. They don't like too much rain – it spoils the fabulous colours of their petals, or too much sun, which makes them fade. They are ideal for the average window box in a city which is probably slightly in the gloom and more often than not overshadowed by the sill from the floor above or by the roof and therefore doesn't get much rain directly on it. That's a point to remember when watering primulas and auriculas, try just to wet the roots and leaves and not the flowers.

Although they look rather choosy and rather artificial – more like cardboard cut-outs from the distance than real plants – auriculas are amazingly hardy and come in fact from alpine country. If your window box is in an exposed position, however, it is better to bring them indoors in midwinter, so grow them in movable pots and bury them in the box so you can get them out again easily. Whatever happens auriculas must be well drained; they hate to be waterlogged, so wait until the soil is almost bone dry before watering. This matters particularly from October onwards when they are resting. It doesn't matter if the outer leaves wither and die but take them off;

Auriculas are ideal for a town window box

never leave half soggy dead leaves around or botrytis, a fungus disease which is a nuisance to get rid of, will set in.

How to stretch space
One-colour gardens, whether they are on a patio or a balcony or even simply in a window box, are a marvellous way of stretching space in a chic way. A mixture of blues, for instance, from forget-me-nots to lobelia can look very good against a cool grey wall – it's important, incidentally, to take the colour of your walls into account when planning a colour scheme. Hot red geraniums, for instance, look awful against hot red brick and the rather gaudy bedding begonia looks gaudier still against this colour scheme – a house in really livid-coloured brick needs cooling with something like silver foliage. One of the most chic plantings I ever saw, in a house in Chelsea, was simply based on greens. There were no flowers at all, the house was painted an immaculate brilliant white, the front door was purple, and the window boxes were painted shiny black and

filled with green plants of every kind, ivy tumbling over the sides, small pieces of box clipped into cones and fresh paler green feathery foliage in between. It's certainly an idea for a trouble-free window box garden, and provided you include some evergreens it works all the year round.

Silver foliage, as I've said, makes a perfect foil for hot-coloured stucco or brick and indeed for a brick paved area in front of the house. Against flagstones silver looks rather insipid; however you can soon remedy that by standing a few pots of ramrod-straight flowers among them – gladioli and montbretia in summer, some of the more exotic lilies like the shocking pink nerines too, and in the spring tulips and hyacinths. The advantage of this kind of gardening is that you have a constant backdrop of silver and can switch the look of the whole garden by adding a few bedding plants here and there at different times of year.

For a silvery carpeting plant try *Lamium galeobdolon* 'Variegatum' which turns out rather unexpectedly to be related to the dead nettle family, although it looks nothing like it. *Stachys* (lambs' ears) has furry, silvery leaves and takes well to a tub, while several of the artemisias – *A. Ludoviciana* and *A. pedemontana lanata*, for instance – are silvery white.

There are, of course, all sorts of shrubs that can be found in silvery colours – even a common privet (*Ligustrum ovalifolium* 'Argenteum'). Both the privet and the Portugal laurel (*Prunus lusitanica*) can be happily turned into trim town trees by simply training them up as standards, pruning ruthlessly in the early stages, then letting them form a ball-like head on top. You can turn almost anything into a standard – even a Michaelmas daisy – and it's well worth doing in formal town surroundings and an easy way to decorate a balcony.

Growing things in tubs
Tub plants are the mainstay of a small back yard, balcony or roof garden because if you have made them portable – more about that later on – they can be shifted around to provide colour exactly where you want it, or to rest up in the months when they are not pretty and productive in a corner somewhere. You have to decide

really which you are going to have with a tub – a cornucopia of flowers and a riot of leaves tumbling down the sides, or an attractive outline. What doesn't work is something between the two. I never rate daffodils or small bulbs very highly in tubs, they look dwarfed by their surroundings – but they make useful underplantings around a small tree in a tub. For sheer show you can't really beat any of the palm family; the hardy varieties are all grouped together under the family names of *Chamaerops* and *Tachycarpus*. *T. fortunei*, the Chusan palm is perfectly hardy anywhere sheltered in Britain and its enormous fan-shaped leaves can grow to 4 ft wide and 2½ ft long. It *has* been known to reach 25 ft in height in this country but that is the exception. Keep it in a tub by your front door and it will be unlikely to reach 5 ft for the tub has a useful effect of miniaturising most trees. *Chamaerops humilis* is an interesting miniature palm that might have been made for a small paved area or a balcony. It's very rarely known to grow more than 5 ft in height and is the palm you see growing wild in some parts of south-west Europe, where it covers the mountain sides by the coast.

Don't forget if you are planning an exotic look that the good old fatsia, *F. japonica*, sometimes incorrectly called the castor oil plant, looks very like the indoor house plant *Monstera deliciosa*, which you

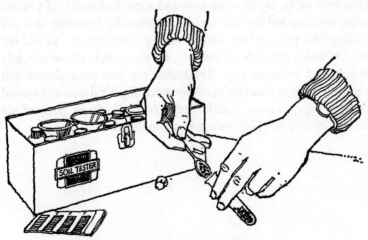

Find out what your soil is lacking

often see growing alongside a rubber plant. It has huge hand-shaped glossy green leaves and the fatsia – once called *Aralia sieboldii* – looks very similar and has one great advantage in a town garden or balcony: although it seems very tropical it in fact likes semi-shade. It's excellent for the seaside where some plants tend to give up under salt-sprayed air. Another shade lover is the hosta, a currently fashionable plant for town gardens with its huge, attractive leaves.

Gardening by the sea

Going back to thoughts of the sea, if you are not going to be disappointed by your window boxes or tubs in a sea-side flat, then it's important if your windows or balcony face a prevailing sea wind to plant the right things. Sea buckthorn (*Hippophae rhamnoides*), which is silver grey, and sea holly (*Eryngium*), which looks like a very exotic version of the Scottish thistle, also has silvery leaves with blue flowers and will grow well on balconies facing the sea; so also will fuchsias, and hydrangeas, lavender and senecio. The soil is vitally important when you are gardening by the sea – what you have around you is probably thin and lacking in humus and either sandy, or salt-laden and boggy if you are anywhere near the Thames Estuary. So it's essential either to import fresh soil from elsewhere or to dig in some peat and some leafmould. If you are using existing soil by the sea, it's worthwhile investing in a soil testing kit – you can buy them at most garden centres – to find out exactly which minerals are missing, for the earth is almost certainly unbalanced in some way. Remember too that your shrubs will probably have to stand up to strong prevailing winds; on an exposed patio it pays to grow a little hedge (even if it's in pots) of sea buckthorn and sea holly to act as a windbreak.

2 Clothing the Walls

CLIMBERS ARE a magnificent means of getting more mileage out of a very small garden, a backyard or a balcony because they give you an extra dimension in colour, will often help to hide an unsightly view and, if you are faced with a blank wall from your window, they'll clothe it for you and turn it into a picture. On a balcony they can be used to soften up the stark outlines of a rail or retaining wall and to hang over the side in a waterfall of colour and interest; don't forget the side wall on a balcony too, the full-height kind that you get in blocks of flats. With the extra shelter that it provides it's possible even to grow the exotic bougainvillea in a tub in summer.

You can, if you're clever, have a display of climbers on the go all year round, even in a confined space, if you pick some for their flowers, some for their foliage – Virginia creeper for instance – and some for winter berries. Most of them can be grown free-standing in tubs or pots if you haven't a bed for them and can't contrive one. If there is a flowerbed available you can double up with shrubs too, for climbers don't compete, and there's no reason, either, why they shouldn't be used as ground cover plants or to cover the top of a tub, for instance, and spill over the sides. Climbers make attractive cut flowers too, for the table; a low spray of clematis at a dinner party is much better than a high bunch of something you can't see round, when you're trying to make conversation.

If you're planning an eating-out area, the simplest pergola can be given an exotic out-of-doors look if you train a vine over it. If you're in a hurry then the mile-a-minute *Polygonum baldschuanicum* will give you shade in the space of one summer, but if you have time to wait a while then you can have a real grape vine, with bunches of grapes dangling over your head – a safer choice since it's not likely to get out of hand, as the Russian vine is prone to do.

Climbers hide an ugly view or disguise an unattractive window

Quick cover-ups

However, if you want to cover a wall quickly, at all costs, then there are several climbers that will help you do it effectively. The two I would pick for a start are the Russian vine and Jack's crazy creeper, more usually known as Virginia creeper. The latter, *Parthenocissus quinquefolia*, to give it its official name, will quickly swarm over walls up chain-link fencing, giving dense coverage. It's self-clinging and in the autumn it turns to a rich crimson shade. It has an even more attractive but slower-growing cousin, incidentally, the beauty basket vine (*Ampelopsis brevipedunculata*) which has greeny silver leaves shot with other colours too, and its real advantage is that it loves a poor dry soil – overfeed it and the leaves will turn to an ordinary green instead. The Russian vine grows with such astonishing rapidity that I could swear you would actually see it at work; it makes lots of side shoots too. It has racemes of attractive small white flowers in midsummer and if you make a practice of pruning it back, as you will need to, to keep it under control, it can develop thick, gnarled vine-like stems, like a real grapevine.

Annual climbers

If you want some quick instant colour on the wall of a balcony or to keep you going while slower climbers establish themselves, then annuals are the answer. Nasturtium – its official name is *Tropaeolum majus* – will scramble all over anything you offer it as a support, can be trained up a Terylene thread or to overhang the rail of a balcony. It will also swarm up wire netting and is, of course, an ideal candidate for planting in pots, window boxes or tubs. The nasturtium musn't have too rich a soil to feed on or it will tend to make all leaves and no flowers. For shade *Tropaeolum speciosum*, a smaller-flowered, perennial climber (the flowers are red) will thrive in an acid soil and not miss the sun, while small varieties of *T. majus*, like 'Golden Gleam' can be kept in a small flower pot and trained up twigs. Morning glory is a good climber to grow if you can give it a good start indoors to get it underway early, for it is only half hardy here. Always soak the seeds overnight in warm water before planting – they're incredibly hard – and remember that it hates being transplanted, so sow it in the pot in which it is going to grow (if you're putting it in the ground then use a paper pot at first).

Another helpful annual is the *Cobaea scandens*, the cup and saucer plant from Central and South America. It is, actually, a perennial but rarely if ever lasts the winter in this country and has to be started off again from seed. It's a vigorous plant that is self-support-ing if you give it a trellis or some sort of frame to cling to and it will achieve heights of as much as 20 ft in one summer. Gourds are useful climbers to grow against a balcony wall and so are moonflowers, and the canary creeper. One annual climber that we tend to forget is the hop (*Humulus*) which will reward you with plenty of good growth. It will cover arches or pergolas rapidly and makes a good windbreak.

Clematis for colour

The stock pop climbers, the ones you'll find at any garden centre, which are guaranteed to give you good value for money in terms of colour are clematis, wisteria and the rose. There are so many varieties of clematis, some of them evergreen, that you could easily clothe the walls of a garden with nothing else, and organise almost year-round flowers too; some of them are very early and others stay flowering until winter arrives. Indeed, if your soil is chalky you couldn't do better than concentrate on these. Despite what you may have heard to the contrary, most clematises are surprisingly good-tempered plants – provided you keep their bases and roots in the shade and see that they get enough water. Most cases of wilting that arise with these plants are due quite simply to lack of moisture. You can easily organise shade either by planting a small evergreen shrub close to it, or by quite simply covering the base of the plant with sacking or a piece of slate or something similar. *C.* × *jackmanii* takes a lot of beating for a bold display of colour, though I'm particularly fond of varieties with even deeper mauve flowers, like 'The President'. However you can find species and varieties of this genus with white flowers, lantern-like yellow ones (*C. tangutica*) and, of course, pinks and blues.

It pays to go to a specialist grower if you're taking clematis at all seriously, and to get advice either from him, or from books on the subject, on pruning. Some need cutting right back, others should be thinned out rather gingerly. It depends entirely on what type they are and when they flower, but remember that every time you prune this plant or cut it back you should at the same time give the roots some fertiliser to work on as they will be stimulated to make new growth. Clematis will grow perfectly happily in tubs and pots but avoid ones made from metal since the soil inside is likely to get too hot for comfort unless it is placed in the shade. The clematis loves lime, and can scarcely get enough of it, so if you have any builder's rubble lying around – dig it in round the base of the plant and watch it thrive! Don't be tempted to put fresh lime on the soil, however, or you will risk killing the plant. Clematis also likes company – it will climb in a complementary way with a rose, for instance, or clothe an unattractive shrub or a dead tree with colour.

Ways with wisteria

Wisteria loves a warm sunny wall or, better still, the chance to grow over something like an arch or a pergola where its beautiful lilac-coloured flowers can be seen to their best advantage, dangling overhead. Sun is really essential for good flowering, and so is pruning – you must cut the stems back in the winter to within a few inches of the old wood. Deal with it in December if you want it to flower well the next year. Do remember, by the way, when you're planning to plant, that it hates too much wind so choose a sheltered corner. Wisteria is relatively self-supporting, since it develops a woody trunk, and can be trained up a living tree without danger of killing it – unless the victim is such a spindly specimen that the sheer weight of wisteria drags it down. I've seen it growing as a companion to a laburnum in a small town garden; the trailing racemes of flowers, lilac blue from the wisteria, yellow from the tree complement each other beautifully.

Roses and honeysuckle

The climbing or rambling roses complete the trio of easy-to-grow colourful plants to clothe a wall. A red rose that goes well on walls is 'Etoile de Hollande'. 'Lemon Pillar' is, as its name suggests, good for using up posts and pergolas, while two old faithfuls that will reward you well if they have enough sun are 'Mme Alfred Carrière' and 'Gloire de Dijon', both suitable for small gardens. Roses can be grown in tubs too – a point that many people tend to forget.

Honeysuckle is a happy choice for a smallish garden and if you want all-year-round cover you can't do better than stick to *Lonicera henryi* which is evergreen, although you sacrifice something in scent. In the shade *Lonicera* × *tellmanniana* has luscious red-veined yellow flowers, while for winter berries stick to the Dutch honeysuckles, *L. periclymenum* 'Belgica' and *L. periclymenum* 'Serotina'.

More colour for the wall

What else will colour your walls well? The Virginia creeper grows splendidly on any wall facing south or west. I used to loathe it heartily, having only seen it grown against red brick where it has the effect of an unpleasant hot flush on the wall in the autumn sun. But I changed my mind completely recently when I saw it growing against a plain white wall. It took on a new, much more chic dimension there; it looks good on grey too. Like ivy, it tends to be tenacious so it shouldn't be allowed to grow anywhere where there is soft crumbling stone – it fastens itself to a wall in a flash by means of its own discs, which makes it very difficult to yank off again. For the same reason you shouldn't let it wander under the eaves of a house or get into the gutters.

If you want a really good show of colour the Chilean glory vine (*Eccremocarpus scaber*) will give you a waterfall of scarlet trumpet-shaped flowers which do equally well in tubs and hanging baskets as against a wall. Plumbago – despite its name which sounds like a disease – gives an exotic, almost tropical look to a balcony or patio wall, provided it has some shelter, with drifts of brilliant blue flowers. A self-clinger that grows in summer and has plenty of scarlet flowers for colour is the trumpet vine, *Campsis radicans*, but it will only perform if it is given warmth and shelter, so that usually means a south-facing wall. Two perennials you might try if you want something more unusual are aristolochia, often called Dutchman's pipe because of the shape of its yellow-brown flowers, and the potato vine which has nothing whatsoever to do with the potato and has bluish-purple flowers.

Temporary help

If your wall hasn't already got strategically placed nails or wires on it, if trellis looks too obtrusive, or you're only passing through and plan to move before long, then try nailing up green nylon netting (Netlon is one make available) and let climbers grow up over that. This is particularly good for the rather delicate ones whose stems are brittle and easily broken and it doesn't show as much as thick wires or wooden slats.

For winter cover

Your wall needn't look bare in the wintertime. This is where ivy comes in so handy, for it's amazingly good tempered, doesn't mind shade and keeps going all year round. It has rather undeservedly got a bad reputation – you would imagine that it could pull a building apart with its bare stems, to hear some people talk about it. But there's no doubt that if the structure of the wall is basically sound ivy will do it no harm at all, and give you a vista of green to look at every month of the year. It makes a good backdrop, too, for more colourful climbers and saves that bare brick look.

You don't have to stick to just plain dark green leaves either. Variegated ivies are already well known as pot plants but there are plenty that will grow out of doors – many can be planted in cracks in a wall halfway up if there is room for a little compost to keep it going, and train down attractively. *Hedera helix* has attractively lobed green leaves. If you want something more exotic try 'Gold Heart' which is a mixture of green and gold or 'Glacier' which is green and silver, and looks wonderful against a grey wall or trailing over a charcoal-grey fibreglass urn. For un-ivy shaped leaves try 'Sagitti-folia' which is quite delicate looking, or 'Green Ripple' which you wouldn't imagine was ivy at all.

Another evergreen that gives good value for money is *Hydrangea integerrima* (you'd never connect it with the shrub, despite its relationship) which has rich glossy dark green leaves though its flowers are nothing much to write home about. For a better display in summer – its large blooms are a creamy white colour of magnolia – *Hydrangea petiolaris* is a self-clinging climber which you could train as a shrub if you changed your mind.

When winter comes two plants that are strictly shrubs but almost behave like climbers, reaching 10 ft or so, will give you flowers just when you need them. Both, incidentally, look good growing against ivy. *Chimonanthus praecox*, the winter sweet, flowers all through December and January, giving you small star-like blooms that are yellow on the outside, scarlet within, and have a sweet scent – cut some and bring it indoors on a winter day and you'll appreciate its heady perfume. *Jasminum nudiflorum* produces very similar flowers but its rather whippy, unprepossessing stalks are best trained against a trellis, otherwise it looks like an unmade bed. This is an easy plant to propagate by the way – just anchor the end of a stalk in the ground and it will root while still attached to the mother plant. You could partner it with *Jasminum officinale* which starts blooming in June and goes on almost until *J. nudiflorum* bursts into flower on its bare branches.

Climbers for difficult spots

No-one is going to complain about having a south-facing wall to clothe with climbers, since the choice is endless, but if your wall faces north you are restricted a little. Honeysuckle is quite happy in the shade; so is *Garrya elliptica* which has attractive green catkins and can be grown as a shrub too. It has one great advantage for it never really needs pruning or cutting back and will go on happily for years. The Chilean coral plant, *Berberidopsis corallina*, will take to a shady wall and cover it with evergreen, dark leaves and coral flowers. Another good candidate for a shady wall is *Akebia quinata* which almost comes into the evergreen category and has unusual brownish-purple flowers. It's a twiner by nature and needs some support. On a west-facing wall a fig tree will flourish, trained against the bricks, and tree paeonies will give you luscious flowers. *Pyracantha*, the firethorn, is good for a wall that faces east and is occasionally plagued by a biting wind. Just train it against the brickwork and it will look after itself. *Hydrangea petiolaris* will cope with an east-facing wall too. If you're lucky enough to have a sheltered south wall you must grow the passion flower (it's good for balconies too) even though you may have to wait up to three years for the blooms to appear. Although I say it likes a south wall best, I've seen it growing at Findhorn in Scotland, way north of Inverness, against an ordinary fence. Its curious, rather formal flowers have decorative filaments that look as though they were painted on; all in all it has a rather waxy look and any allusion to passion is religious rather than romantic.

How to make a hanging garden

There are other ways to clothe a wall than using climbers but, while I'm on the subject, don't forget that what goes up can come down – and in that case you can do away with supports. Troughs firmly anchored on the top of a high brick wall can be used to house clematis and any of the colourful climbers and annuals like nasturtiums or morning glories so that they cascade down the wall, and you could have more trained up to meet them from below. This

Clematis trails down gracefully from a wall-mounted trough

scheme only works if the wall is sheltered, otherwise in a windy place you would have to secure them. You could have a positive hanging garden of Babylon if you planted shrubs and climbers at the base of a tall wall, trailers cascading from the top, *and* strategically placed half-baskets and troughs of flowers dotted in between.

Another idea for a small wall – possibly the end of a balcony – is to fix identical flower pots at carefully spaced intervals dotted all over it with, say, geraniums or fuchsias growing in them, to give the effect almost of a floral wallpaper. A low retaining wall can be clothed with other things than climbers. If it has any convenient cracks in it you can poke in an alpine or two, cottage flowers like wallflowers, stocks, antirrhinum will thrive too if you push in the seeds and cover with a little soil. To cheat a little, provided the wall is sound, loosen the mortar in places with a metal knitting needle or a skewer and put a little compost in. Dianthus does well in and on walls, so does night-scented stock (*Matthiola bicornis*) and valerian (*Centranthus ruber*) with deep pink, star-shaped flowers – you can see it used this way in the garden of the Grey Friars at Canterbury. It has the great advantage of a long flowering season. The succulents, cotyledon (often referred to as wall pennywort) and sempervivum thrive in walls, too, and so do the sedums and of course ivies.

Training a shrub

You can induce almost any shrub to make a decent covering for a small wall if you train it. Cut any branches that threaten to grow forward, make it grow as much like a fan as possible and plant it close to its neighbour; that way you can force it to change its shape from round and shrubby to tall and thin. *Euonymus japonicus*, the spindle tree with its greeny-white flowers and glossy dark leaves can be persuaded to grow this way; fuchsias respond to training too. *Cotoneaster horizontalis* will support itself erect, standing there in its rather stiff way with its waxy leaves and red berries, so will *Pyracantha* which is freer and less regimental in shape but has equally attractive berries. This is not a good shrub for a very narrow bed in a courtyard, though, for when the berries drop they tend to get trodden into the flagstones and make a fearful mess. *Erica carnea*, the good-tempered winter-flowering heath that doesn't really mind a chalk or clay soil, looks good in a winter garden, flowers early and has pale pink bell-like flowers that go well with the red berries of *Cotoneaster* or the yellow of winter jasmine. *Rhododendron praecox* will also give you flowers at a time of the year when you need colour.

Camellias for corners

Provided you can give it an acid soil, or dose your existing soil with peat dug in, and the addition of Sequestrine for iron, a camellia makes an attractive addition to the corner of a wall. It loves shade and grows beautifully in tubs and looks very good in a formal garden or patio, mixed with rhododendrons and azaleas. The x *williamsii* hybrids are the safest choice for reliability with their pink flowers like full-blown roses. They shed their own petals too, an advantage since camellias should really be dead-headed if they are to give a good display of blooms.

Cover your wall with fruit

An idea for making practical use of a wall and clothing it at the same time is to line it with espalier-trained fruit trees, choosing something slightly more exotic and unusual than you might normally buy. Nectarines, for instance, morello cherries (which are almost unobtainable now in the shops) or quince could all be persuaded to decorate a wall and give you a bonus of fruit.

The grape vine is another obvious choice. Don't go for 'Black Hamburg' out of doors, it really does need glass to ripen its luscious grapes. But there are a number of new varieties now that thrive out of doors, some of which produce white grapes that can be used either for eating or for wine-making (one vine should yield about 4 bottles of wine). Madeleine Angevine is good for this. I have one trained against the wall of our house which has only been transplanted this year, a process that usually sets them back. But it has several heavy bunches of grapes hanging from the lower branches.

For effect – perhaps to train over a pergola in an eating-out area, to give a Mediterranean look, you can't do better than buy one of the German varieties like 'Faber' (which grows fast on a clay soil) or 'Reichensteiner' (which makes a very fine wine). 'Brandt' is another fast grower, but the grapes are not of a very good quality. You can grow a grape vine now in any sort of soil you choose except a very waterlogged one. Most plants offered for sale are grafted on to American rootstocks as a precaution against phylloxera, so you can literally pick a rootstock to suit your particular ground.

One slightly more unusual fruit you can grow is the Chinese gooseberry, *Actinidia chinensis*, which has small, creamy-white flowers in midsummer, followed by curious hairy fruits which are very pleasant to eat. The Chinese gooseberry hates chalk but it will take to partial shade. If you want to be sure of a crop buy two plants, one male one female, to ensure pollination.

One last thought: for a quick and edible wall covering, you really can't beat the good old runner bean which will reach 8-10 ft easily and can be persuaded to grow up netting. If you feel that the traditional scarlet flowers are too tell-tale, then try 'Sunset', a new variety which is salmon pink.

3 Choosing and Planting your Window Box

WINDOW BOXES come in all shapes and sizes it's true, but it's usually my sad experience that they never ever quite fit *your* window neatly. However, despite that, I wouldn't advise anyone to go to the trouble of making some for themselves unless it is absolutely necessary – it's a fiddly, time-consuming, messy business, especially if you live in a flat. The box needs to be very strongly made or the weight of the damp soil inside it will burst its sides and being made of wood it will start to deteriorate almost as soon as you put it out on the window sill, however much preservative you paint on.

If you find yourself with an impossible-sized sill to fit, there is one simpler solution – fix a supporting bracket at the side in each corner, where the edge of the sill and the outside wall join up and meet at right angles. Fix a brightly-painted plank across on these brackets, turning your sill into a kind of trough. Now place a

Treatment for an awkward window sill

row of flower pots behind it – if the plank is wide enough it will have the same appearance as a well-fitting window box and the pots won't show behind it. And you will also have the advantage of being able to switch your pots around as you will, a much more flexible, less messy arrangement for anyone who relies on bought bedding plants for window sill colour.

Ready-made boxes

Of the ready-mades available – and I must warn you that, taken in bulk, if you are doing several window sills, they turn out to be surprisingly expensive – there's no doubt that plastic is the most practical proposition. But most of the plastic troughs you'll see around are an unpleasant bath-tub shape and either in municipal green or black. Look further – I found some eventually (made by Harcostar) which are white with a roughened look of cement about them. They're deep enough to take a good display of flowers, anything anyone would want to plant and they are sponged white and clean in a minute, which is a godsend in the polluted atmosphere of a town. The kind of window box to avoid if your windows face south or west, is the type made from metal, since they become baking hot in the sun and tend to dry and fry their contents. Plastic on the other hand tends to retain moisture which is a good thing. Don't forget the weight factor – it's difficult enough lugging even a small plastic box filled with earth across a room and out on to a sill and even worse in a way if you are doing it from the outside and have to lift it up. Of course you could put it in place and then fill it, but that makes an appalling mess. How people ever get those decorative stone window boxes into place I'll never know.

Be sure it's safe

Is your box secure? That's not as silly as it seems for most sills are made to slope slightly to allow rainwater to run off, and disasters *could* occur; what the damages would be for a heavy window box crashing down on a passer-by's head I don't dare think. If your sill is shallow or sloping it's vital to secure the box in some way, either with brackets at the side or something underneath. I have mine on tiny blocks fixed to the sill for two reasons: safety and drainage. And watering is another problem – go carefully if you are up high or you'll shower the street.

If you've an opening casement window you may think that a window box is ruled out but it isn't, although you have to go to more trouble; boxes can be fixed on supporting brackets on the wall so that their tops come flush with the window sill and you just brush over the flowers when you open the window. Sash windows are easier of course. Here you can, if you like, use a window box and its contents as a kind of café curtain to screen a view of what is going on in a room. This is particularly good in the case of a bathroom where you don't want to put up a net curtain or a blind; a bank of green coming halfway up the lower sash window acts as a perfect café curtain.

Making your own boxes
If you are making your own window boxes – and it's certainly the cheapest way of doing things – remember to keep the length within bounds; if you've got a wide window you'll probably have to make two or even three to sit into the space. About 3 ft long is the

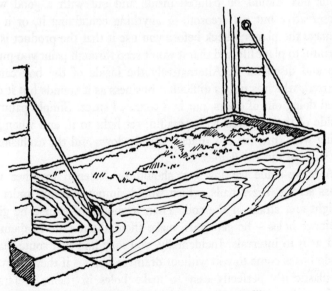

Anchoring a window box on a narrow sill

maximum you can handle when it is full of earth, without the whole thing becoming unwieldly and possibly distorted. Softwood – deal or pine – is usually used for window box construction but if you can afford hardwood the box will last longer. If you can find some well-weathered planks of wood, so much the better.

You'll naturally tailor the width of the box to fit the size of the sill, but you can't really do anything very much with a box that is less than 6 in wide and the depth should be about 10 in – more if it looks better that way. Remember the deeper and wider you can make your box, the less watering will need to be done since a larger bulk and area of soil will retain moisture better than a smaller one. Also, when feeding a box with liquid fertiliser, you are less likely to overdo things and upset the balance of nutriment and minerals in the earth inside. What if your sill is really narrow? With a little trouble you can use a wider window box – but in that case it's necessary to support it with metal bars fixed on the window above it, so that it hangs in place to a certain extent.

Preparation

Your box should be painted inside and out with a good wood preservative but *not* creosote or anything containing it, or it will damage the plants; check before you use it that the product is not harmful to plant life and that it won't seep through paint you put on top and discolour it. Alternatively the inside of the box can be charred, which is not as difficult a business as it sounds but it does need doing out of doors, not in a confined space. Simply paint the inside of the box well with paraffin, set light to it, and when it is going well, turn the box quickly upside down and the exclusion of air will put out the flames.

A home-made window box should be fastened together with brass screws, *never* nails, which would simply pull out under the weight and strain of the soil. Then it should of course be given drainage holes – be generous, make them about 1 in. in diameter and at 9 in intervals. Incidentally, you may find that some ready-made boxes come to you without drainage holes – if they are wood or plastic it's perfectly easy to make holes in them, preferably with an electric drill. You can drill asbestos too, but tin and stone need an expert touch. Finally your home-made box needs at least three coats of paint, preferably four if it is made from softwood. Give it one coat of primer, then two of undercoat and finally a topcoat. That way it will last you a long time.

Now comes the time to fill it. You don't have to worry about a window box getting waterlogged as a rule; if it is anywhere in the sun evaporation will take care of any water that is not absorbed by the roots. However, in a dank, rainy period the soil could become sour and unpleasant, so start off with a small layer of drainage material such as pieces of broken crockery or clay pot. Place the pieces over the bottom, making sure that you put one over each drainage hole so that it does not become clogged up. Then unless your box is in an exposed position where it will get rained on a great deal (check this, because on some parts of our house the window boxes are so well protected that they don't get any share at all of the rain that is going) add a thin scattering of cinders or small pebbles or ashes, then add another layer of moss or turf laid upside down – this will help to keep the roots moist.

Mixing the soil

What kind of soil should you use? A lot of people make a mistake and decide they will give their box the very best and buy some John Innes Compost No 1 – but this mixture is too light in fertiliser. If you're going to this expense then you want the stronger John Innes No 3. Since plants in a box rather than in the open soil are leading a rather unnatural life, they need the best possible quality soil that you can give them. Don't just dig a sackful from someone's garden and leave it as it is; in the first place, you'll end up with a fine crop of weeds and weeding is something we don't want to have to do in window boxes, and in the second place it will probably be unpleasantly stony. Use garden soil by all means, but sieve it first and sort it over. If you can, let it dry out completely, when it is much easier to sort out the stones and weeds. An ideal mixture for a window box would be a combination of some John Innes No 3 and some ordinary garden soil with a little crushed charcoal added to keep it sweet. If the soil is inclined to be heavy

39

and sticky then you can mix in some peat to lighten it. But remember, if there is any quantity of peat in the soil it needs to be thoroughly soaked before any planting is done, and kept moist at all times; it tends to dry out before other types of growing medium.

Choosing your plants

It is important to choose plants which have a good chance of thriving in window box conditions. The trouble with window boxes is that they are so *public*, you're on show the whole time and a row of brownish wilting flowers screams neglect for all the world to see. I found this when I planted some west-facing boxes with primroses, which really prefer woodland conditions. I dug them up from our field because they were cheap and 'instant' and I had a lot of boxes to fill. But I would come home every afternoon and find they had all flopped in the spring sunshine and needed dowsing in water, and my shame was there for everyone in the street to see. Now I've transferred them to a small bed in a courtyard and they are much much happier.

What you plant in your boxes depends on what time you have. There are some good old stayers which can be depended upon for colour all through the summer and although they may seem to be a hackneyed choice for trouble-free window boxes they can't be beaten. Take geraniums (*Pelargonium*) for instance. The choice is enormous from the vigorous bedding plant 'Paul Crampel' with its crimson flowers to the lovely little miniature 'Vesuvius' which is ideal for very small or shallow window boxes and has dark red flowers. You can happily fill a window box with a mixture of standards at the back and trailing ivy-leafed geraniums at the front but it would be expensive, so it usually pays to infiltrate a few in the first year, then take cuttings to increase your stock for the next season. Geraniums will winter perfectly happily by the way, if taken indoors. What usually kills them is over-enthusiastic watering. The soil should be kept only just moist, which means once-a-week watering at most. If you are shifting them into pots, use plastic ones if you can as they hold water longer. Remove any stumps or shoots that have become shrunken and blackened.

Taking a geranium cutting

The best time to take cuttings is during July and August – if you leave it as late as September they won't have a chance to root properly before winter comes. Taking cuttings is a good way to encourage the plant to become bushy and avoid that ungainly straggly, wooden look that elderly geraniums sometimes get. To take a cutting just take off the top part of a stem with very sharp scissors or, better still, a razor blade, cleanly just above the fourth leaf down. Then trim the cutting back to below the third leaf joint, taking off the bottom pair of leaves and dip it into the correct hormone powder to help it root. For preference, use a powder with a fungicide built into it as geraniums are prone to disease at this stage for with a thick stem it has quite a large wound to heal over. Leave the cutting to grow in a pot of sharp sand.

Another method of propagation that works particularly well on a window sill indoors is to stick the cuttings in a jar of liquid solution such as Phostrogen, so that they can grow in water (see Chapter 9 for more about hydroponic methods). You can actually watch the roots growing, through the glass, and once they are well-established, the cutting can be potted on to continue growing. By careful use of cuttings and looking after your stock in winter, you can easily quadruple your supply of geraniums in one year, which makes furnishing window boxes with them quite a cheap proposition in the long run. Geraniums should be put out once the frosts have finished – usually the end of May and taken in again in the autumn when there's a danger of frost again.

Begonias and petunias

Another good colourful stayer for a window box is the bedding begonia – not the perennial bulbous type but the annual grown from seed. They come in a harlequin set of colours, some with green leaves, some with leaves of a purply-brown; the flowers range from sugar pink to white and scarlet, will stand up to drought well and will go on all through the summer. A tray of these won't cost you very much and is a good investment. Although usually treated as annuals, they are half-hardy perennials and will winter indoors; cuttings are easily taken. Petunias with their vivid flowers are another good safe choice for a colourful window box and don't need much attention. They're easy to buy in bedding form from any garden centre in early summer and keep going for months. The other good-tempered long lasting plant for a box is the fuchsia which can be bought in pendulous or upright forms, gives a profusion of flowers and can be overwintered in the same way as geraniums.

Other suitable plants

Fuchsias flourish in shady places, and so do tuberous-rooted begonias, which are a godsend in a window box that is always in shadow. So are violas, pansies and calceolarias. Alyssum and lobelia are perhaps a rather hackneyed choice now for window boxes but there's a lot to be said for them in terms of brightness and cheapness. What else looks good? Antirrhinums and wall-flowers, cornflowers, cinerarias and centaureas give interest in the form of foliage, then there are marguerites and heliotrope. I have had great success with anemones too, and it is easy to tuck the tiny corms in between other growing plants and let them come up. Nasturtiums are a godsend in terms of colour and will trail very attractively over the side. Forget-me-nots are pretty to plant, if you are able to see them close to, and go well mixed with some of the more usual silvery-leafed geraniums for a cool-looking colour combination. Plants that are normally kept indoors will love a spell out in a box in midsummer and put on an enormous amount of growth. Another happy thought for a window box is the miniature rose, which can look very pretty indeed.

Turn your box into a greenhouse

Annuals can be tiresome to grow *in situ* since they take so long to get away and meanwhile your box is going to look bald. You can give them a head start, though, by turning the box into a miniature greenhouse. You can do this in two ways: either cover it with transparent polythene, making sure that it can't come in contact with the seedlings and scorch them, and up-end jam jars over the seedlings as they come up, or do what I've done, get some off-cuts of that corrugated clear plastic roofing material and push it in so

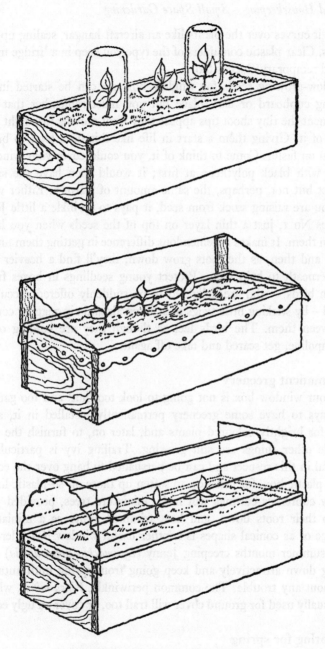

Ways of creating a miniature greenhouse

that it curves over the plants like an aircraft hangar, sealing up the ends. Clear plastic containers of the type you keep in a 'fridge make good temporary cloches too.

Slow-growing seeds for window box use can be started in an airing cupboard or dark place but you must remember that the moment the tiny shoot tips appear they want moving into light and lots of it. Giving them a start in life like this does tend to bring them on faster. Come to think of it, you could cover your window box with black polythene at first; it would then have the same effect but not, perhaps, the same amount of warmth. Either way, if you are raising stock from seed, it pays to sprinkle a little John Innes No 1, just a thin layer on top of the seeds when you have sown them. It makes a tremendous difference in getting them under way and then, as the roots grow down, they'll find a heavier soil underneath to help them. Protect young seedlings in boxes from town birds – who are delighted to be suddenly offered succulent food – by sticking little twigs in at intervals and zig-zagging cotton between them. The birds feel as though they are landing on a trampoline, get scared and take off again.

Permanent greenery

If your window box is not going to look too 'hot' and too gaudy, it pays to have some greenery permanently installed in it, as a foil for brightly coloured plants and, later on, to furnish the box while other things are still growing. Trailing ivy is particularly useful in this respect and can be persuaded to hang over the edges of a plastic box, for instance, to soften up those oh-so-plastic lines. Tiny cupressus cuttings will make miniature trees, provided you keep their roots down, and box, trimmed either as a miniature hedge or as conical shapes is another useful window box filler. In the summer months creeping Jenny (*Lysimachia nummularia*) will hang down attractively and keep going from spring until autumn without any trouble. The common periwinkle, *Vinca minor*, which is usually used for ground cover will trail too, or cover an ugly edge.

Planting for spring

Come September or October, it's time to think of the winter ahead and decide what to plant. Now is the moment to install bulbs for next spring. Ramrod rows of tulips give the most flower power, but it's a shame just to confine yourself to these when there are so many other things available. I'm particularly fond of the more ragged parrot tulips with their interesting colourings, but there are lots of others too. For a small box miniature daffodils like the 'hoop petticoat' (*Narcissus bulbocodium*) look good or for early flowering, 'glory of the snow' (*Chionodoxa*) goes well with crocuses and snowdrops for a very early display. Remember that your bulbs must stay put until all their greenery has died down. It's dangerous to lift them before or they may not come up again next year. This is where a little permanent greenery helps; ivy or box will veil from the passer-by's eye the yellowing foliage behind, before you've got your fresh supply of plants in.

Don't forget that a window box doesn't necessarily have to be on a window. I've seen them placed on a low wall to give extra colour and interest; they look good, too, placed up the side of a flight of basement steps, attached to a balcony by stout metal brackets or hung on walls. Don't forget that you can grow vegetables, herbs and fruit in them (see Chapter 6). There's nothing more rewarding than leaning our of your own window and picking a handful of tiny tomatoes for instance, or helping yourself to some sprigs of mint.

4 Planning your Patio

IF YOU think of a patio as an outdoor room, that's the best way to plan one – whether it's forming part of a roof garden or simply jazzing up a back yard. It's amazing what you can do to make a sitting-out area look attractive with the minimum effort. One of the nicest ones I've ever seen was copied from a French café and involved little or no structural work at all – wooden troughs containing full-grown box hedging were put on either side to shut out unattractive fences and it was fronted by similar troughs with

Turn your patio into a French café

clipped conifers in them. The owners had bought a gaily striped shop blind and had it fitted to the back of the house, so that it pulled down over the patio for shade and shelter and made it possible for them to eat outside for a great deal of the year. Now you can buy special outdoor heaters (they first used them in Sweden) which will even give a warm glow to a patio, provided there is some sort of roof cover.

Another idea for an eating out place is to build a simple pergola with timber uprights and a roof of widely placed planks laid on

A vine-covered pergola provides a roof for
an eating out place

end, then plant a quick-growing vine up it and cover the whole thing in with a blue-tinted translucent plastic top. Once the vine has established itself the plastic will be almost unnoticeable – you'll imagine it is a clear blue sky above. This sort of setting, too, would lend itself to outdoor heating, and the variety of special lights to go in patios of this kind is endless now, ranging from what look like flaming torches to oil lamps or hurricane lamps wired for electricity. My favourite type is flood-lighting hidden among the plants and highlighting creepers and a magnolia, say, or a palm. At night this gives even the most humble patio a really exotic air.

First fix the floor

First things first, and it's important to decide on the flooring and walls for your outdoor room, even if you are simply cutting off part of a yard so that when you sit out you don't have to see the dustbins. A wall made from second-hand bricks covered with ivy can give even the newest patio an old-world air and go very well with country cottages. For the floor, brickwork, like pebbles, should be used sparingly, if your patio is exposed to the elements, for these become lethally slippery after rain or if moss is allowed to take a hold. For all round cheapness and safety you can't really beat concrete, and it comes in so many different colours and shapes now that that old pale grey, rather dingy look is no longer necessary. The nicest terraces are made from pre-cast concrete flagstones (you can get them in 18 in or 2 ft squares) or some of the more fancy shapes like hexagonal, fitted together. Sometimes a mixture of squares and rectangles or several slabs of different colour and texture can be mixed with great effect. Another useful way of using two colours of concrete is to define an eating-out area on a terrace, using different coloured stones, or you could make the level slightly higher at that end.

How to lay a terrace

If you can't afford the expense of ready-made slabs, if your patio is of an awkward shape, or if you want to incorporate several features such as planting areas and a tiny pool into it, then you can easily lay a terrace for yourself that looks as though it is made from separate flagstones but is in fact in one piece. For this you need a mixture of 1 part cement, 2½ parts sand, and 4 parts coarse aggregate – measured in the same container by volume, not weight. Use something for mixing it on that can be removed for washing down; once concrete has set it is very difficult to shift, so do your stirring up on an old door or a piece of board.

Mix the cement, the sand and the aggregate, adding water sparingly; use a watering can for the job to prevent it running off in rivulets and keep it under control. The best way to do this is rather like mixing batter for a pudding – make a hole in the centre of the dry ingredients, pour some water in and add the material from the sides gradually. Keep on turning it over with a spade until no dry material remains. Remember the drier the concrete is, the sooner it will harden and the more tough it will be. If you are doing a large area, then your local hire shop will be able to lend you a mini-mixer which will save you a lot of time. The Cement and Concrete Association, 52 Grosvenor Gardens, London SW1 have a useful booklet called *Concrete in Garden Making* which not only gives you some ideas for patios, steps and other things, but also has a useful chart which helps you to calculate how much concrete you will need for a given area.

It's important to give your terrace a firm base for the concrete to cling to, and about 6 in of compacted hardcore or rubble is best. And remember, you can buy coloured cement as well as plain, so you needn't miss out on that side of things if you are making it yourself. Another point to bear in mind is that you must not cover up the damp course of a building (usually a piece of slate or something that looks like roofing felt inserted between two courses of bricks) or you will have trouble with rising damp. Your concrete covering should be 3 in thick and you can make it look like flagstones by two methods. You can divide it up into a grid using string and pegs, then using boards to mark the shape of the squares as you lay the concrete; remove the boards after it has settled a little. Or you can lay part of the terrace and, using string and pegs for accuracy, divide the concrete up into squares with the edge of a board about an hour after it has been laid, when it is firmish but has not set. In either case a thin dribble of liquid concrete in a darker colour can be carefully poured between the 'flagstones' to increase their effect; alternatively earth could be compacted in, though if you did this, you wouldn't be able to wash it down later.

If you want to add decorative cobbles in some squares you should prepare beds of mortar about 2 in thick, push the cobbles in so that they stand up about $\frac{1}{2}$ in above the surface, then brush in a mixture of 1 part of cement to 3 of sand to finish them off; the cobbles can be cleaned up afterwards with water and a brush.

Making concrete troughs

If you are not planting directly on to the terrace with allowance made for flower-beds, then it's a good idea to cast concrete troughs of the same-coloured cement to go along the sides. You can do this by using pre-cast blocks for the sides surrounding a specially mixed base (1 part cement, 8 parts aggregate) concreted 3 in thick. The slabs are then bedded in mortar, the corners kept together with

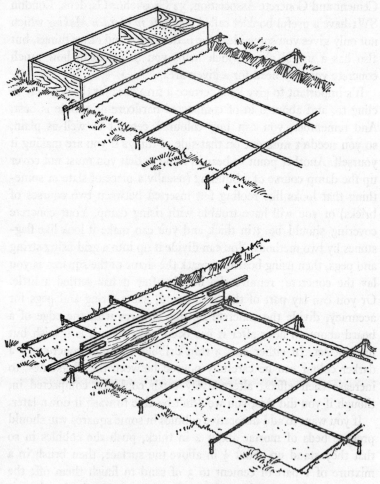

Two ways of creating the effect of flagstones

surgical tape, then filled in with more mortar to sandwich them together. The side slabs should be sunk slightly into the ground for stability.

Another way to cast your own concrete troughs is to find or make two boxes of the same shape, one 2-3 in larger than the other and the outside one the size you want your finished trough to be. Pour about 3 in. of concrete mix in the base of the larger box, sit the smaller one carefully on top, making quite sure that it is centred properly, then shovel in more concrete round between the two sides, making sure you don't leave any air holes. Pieces of tubing inserted just above ground level through the outer box and into the side of the inner one, will provide you with drainage holes. When the concrete has set, just strip off the wood and you have a ready-made trough.

Talking of drainage, remember when laying a terrace that it should slope very slightly *away* from the house, not enough to be noticeable but enough to ensure that water dripping from containers and rain runs away in the direction of the garden and doesn't linger in little waterlogged patches.

Crazy paving

Crazy paving is another choice for a patio of course but it's likely to drive *you* crazy, fitting the pieces together like a jigsaw, and tends to go with garden gnomes in a decoration scheme. However, if it's crazy paving you want, buy some ordinary slabs, put them on a bed of mortar, then get a strong friend to shatter them with a pick-axe *in situ*, so that the shapes they make coincide with each other. Using this quick but rather drastic method you'll find you will have to level up the pieces or some will be sticking up like broken teeth. That's the trouble about crazy paving – edges tend to jut up, and trip people, however hard you may try to keep them smooth and even.

Lighting and heating

Don't forget at the floor stage to think in terms of electric light and heat. To avoid electrocuting yourself – and it can happen however careful you are – it's best to engage the help of a qualified electrician.

Outdoor installations need things like waterproof plugs to make them safe, and he might want to bury some wiring in a conduit in the concrete before it is set. Don't forget, too, that if you are planning on a small fountain you'll need an electricity supply for that and it looks less obtrusive buried in a wall or in the ground.

Treatment for an ugly wall

Having got the floor of your patio fixed, then it's time to pay attention to the subject of walls. This depends on what your view is. Do you have dustbins to screen? Are you overlooked by your neighbours? Do you want a feeling of being closed in, of intimacy, or do you want the great outdoors to be seen? Many terraces are bounded by walls on either side which is a great saving in money, but if the wall is not what you like, or possibly not high enough, or just an unattractive fence, it pays to clothe it with creepers as quickly as possible. A too-short wall can have a piece of squared-off trellis fixed on the top for the creeper to continue its journey up.

If the wall in itself is unattractive looking – festooned with pebble dash or made from dingy wooden palings – a trellis is the quickest way to jazz it up. You can buy it now in an enormous variety of widths but remember its actual size depends entirely on how much you unfold it – it can be made much wider if you don't use it at its full height or stretched upwards it becomes much narrower. Either way, fix it securely to the wall with screws or nails, depending on what the wall is made of. Don't just hook it up in place on an old nail, for it catches the wind like a sail and crashes down easily, bringing your treasured plants with it – I've just lost some sunflowers that way.

Painting a trellis

Paint your trellis before you fix it up. This is a time-consuming and messy business and could be made much easier if only one had a large vat of paint in which to dip the thing. One day no doubt someone will come up with ready-coloured plastic trellis, but for the present you just have to cope with it. Don't creosote it first, or the brown will come through anything you put on afterwards. Use a good quality outdoor paint – emulsion is fine – and first paint your

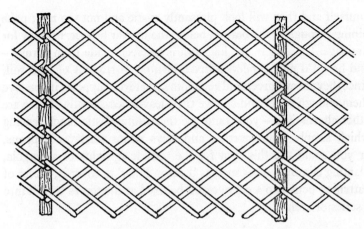

Easy way to join strips of trellis

trellis all over when it is still closed up; put it on newspapers on a table or on a piece of hardboard or planking, because it makes a terrible mess. Let the paint soak in well, and almost dry, then open up your trellis to the size at which it will eventually be hung and fill in all the unpainted gaps with a small brush. It's important to make sure you have it opened to its finished size, otherwise if you stretch it still more, unpainted wood will appear.

You don't have to paint your trellis white – in fact it's become something of a cliché to do so. I've seen it painted a vivid (not municipal) leaf green which made it look marvellous against a dull wall, almost like a creeper. If you are using several strips of trellis, unless you can line up the diamonds perfectly – and that takes some doing and some nailing and screwing – then put strips of plain batten between each sheet, like a wooden column. You could always put a thick post between them so that it looks as if it *is* a column or paint some plastic drain pipe white and use that for a three-dimensional effect – particularly good in a period house.

Dividing off your patio

For the outer wall that faces the rest of the yard, the garden or even the street in some cases, you can easily make a low retaining wall for yourself from bricks. Get hold of some old ones, lay them

53

yourself and they will look pleasantly rustic and not too raw; poke piping through at the bottom before the mortar has set, to allow for drainage. Cheaper in the long run is a screen made from shrubs – and here I'd pick rhododendrons, planted in troughs of acid soil, since they are evergreen and keep going whatever happens, if you give them enough water and sponge their leaves occasionally. There are other alternatives – you could use that white plastic ranch fencing which simply slots together and stays white whatever happens, or you could use this spot for the outside uprights of a pergola, planting climbing roses such as 'Lemon Pillar' to cover it; pieces of battening bent into a curve could be fixed at the top to turn it into a series of arches.

A pierced concrete wall

Or again, you could use one of the dozens of designs of pierced concrete blocks that there are around. They are easily laid and usually come with matching pilasters and posts for extra stability. Measure up carefully beforehand because you simply cannot split one of these blocks in half; you have to make sure that a set of whole ones will fit into the space that you want. First make a firm foundation for a pierced concrete wall by digging out a shallow 9 in trench, then fill it with a concrete footing using the mixture I described for making a terrace (in fact it could all be done at the same time as you lay your terrace). Make sure, whatever you do, that the surface of the trench is level, using a spirit level to check.

You can normally have a 10 ft width of wall without using concrete uprights and since you're not likely in a tiny back yard to have more than this without a gateway you should be able to get away without one. If not, you must take it into your initial calculations. If you are using pilasters, or even uprights built from brick, these should be put up first, checking carefully that you have left space for the blocks between them. As a mortar to bed pierced concrete blocks in place you need a mixture of 1 part cement and 3 parts sand, the usual mortar used between bricks in a garden wall. Wait until your concrete base has set, then spread some of the mortar over this and lay your first block, spreading mortar on the base and side edges. Now fix the second block along side it, mortaring it in the same way, and so on until your first course is laid. Use a plumb line and spirit level as you go to check the levels as nothing is more noticeable than a patterned wall that is apparently leaning over or gone askew. Don't lay too many courses at one time – never attempt a whole wall without letting the concrete on some of it set; brush away surplus mortar with an old paint brush. The manufacturer of the blocks is bound to supply you with a leaflet on their use but that, basically is how it is done.

Building a barbecue

While you are doing brickwork on a terrace it's a good idea to build yourself a barbecue at one end. Really, all you need is a grid of iron over a space into which you can pile coals and charcoal – two heaps of bricks with an old oven-grid placed over them will do. But it's rather nicer to build it in, perhaps on an end wall, for a neater, more thought-out effect. You can also incorporate an area for preparing the food, either using brickwork with concrete slabs on it, a piece of thick slate, or best of all, the top of an old marble wash-stand. More elaborate barbecues can have a hollow square brick pillar at one end with a wooden door fixed in the centre, so that it can be used as a fuel store. Simply build a single-brick wall in a square but lay only a bottom layer at the front, let the edges of the side bricks make the sides of the wall and put a stout piece of wood across the top (this can be covered with concrete in the front) and then a piece of slate or marble for the top. You then cut a simple door to fit, hinged to a batten on the side.

A built-in barbecue for your terrace

The cooking part of the barbecue consists merely of a wall at the back with ledges at either side to take an iron grid on which to cook your food – an old-fashioned grid type shoe-scraper would do for this, a grid tray out of an old oven, or just spaced iron rods set into concrete in the wall on either side. If the fire is to be made from charcoal, then you need an iron tray fixed about 12 in under the grid on ledges in a similar way. If you are using logs of wood, you can slightly raise the floor level on a concrete slab and make your fire lower down.

Furnishing your patio

Patio furniture needs to be either light enough to stowaway – those cane chairs from the East look lovely but take up a dickens of a lot

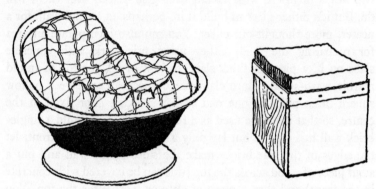

Add a sag-bag to an old hip-bath or a square cushion to a simple cube
for elegant patio furniture

of room indoors – or durable enough to leave out at all times of year. I have not seen any plastic furniture that I can bear, as yet, and wood – even teak – tends to go an unpleasant greyish colour when exposed to the elements. The best things I've found so far are those made from white-painted cast aluminium to old Victorian designs. The only trouble with them is that they are extremely uncomfortable to sit on and need cushions.

Another type of patio furniture that can be very easily made is a simple wooden cube with a small piece of battening round the edge into which you slip a custom-made cushion. Now that you can buy giant sag-bags and other monster cushions ready made up, some merely needing loose covers, home-made patio furniture is not as difficult as it sounds. Someone I know managed to get hold of two old-fashioned tin hip-baths, painted them bright orange and filled them with orange print sag-bags and they look very exotic indeed on her terrace.

Do fit in a pool, somewhere, even if it's merely a fountain unit placed in an urn. There's something very soporific about water splashing down on a patio (provided it isn't coming down on your head, as it could well be in a rainstorm).

How to use hanging baskets
When it comes to choosing patio plants, there's an endless choice, for in this sheltered atmosphere you can grow half-hardy things and

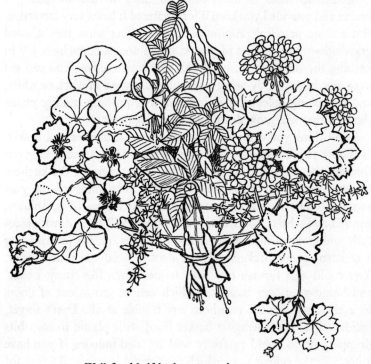

Wall-fixed half-baskets are easier to manage
than the hanging kind

with the extra space available go above window box size in your planting. I mention some shrubs and trees later on – and any shrub that you would plant in a back garden will thrive here, but now is the time to talk about hanging baskets. If they are properly planted they make a quite delightful addition to a patio but remember first of all one point about watering them: *don't* climb up a step ladder and use a watering can – not only will you make a mess but you won't really succeed in soaking them properly. There's only one way to water a hanging basket and that is to immerse it thoroughly in a bucket. This needs doing frequently, as it has so much exposed surface to dry out, so make it easy to detach from the ceiling or the wall. Half-baskets are in a way more practical for a terrace – you don't have anything dangling over your head, they retain moisture better and are usually easier to unhook.

Sphagnum moss is the traditional thing to use for lining a basket and provided you keep it well watered it looks very attractive. But a more practical proposition now is either some turves, used grass-side-out or a sheet of plastic which does a marvellous job in keeping the moisture in, but looks very unattractive. You can get over this, however, by using green plastic instead of black or white, and by poking holes in it at intervals and pushing trailing plants through that will grow down and help disguise it.

Don't think you can only have conventional flowers in a basket. It is easy to plant one in September with bulbs – some poking out through the sides, and if one end of your patio fronts the kitchen, to have one full of herbs which you can keep going all the year round. Otherwise the old favourites such as ivy-leafed geraniums, pendulous fuchsias, lobelia and nasturtiums will hang down gracefully and give you plenty of colour. Ivy helps out too in providing a constant green background and doesn't need too much water. You could also furnish one with house plants like 'busy Lizzie' and 'mind-your-own business' which can be grown out of doors in a sheltered situation without any trouble at all. Don't forget, incidentally, that a hanging basket lined with plastic to stop bits dropping down could perfectly well be used indoors, if you have a hook on the ceiling from which to suspend it or a wall fixing for a half-basket.

John Innes No 3 is as good a compost as any to use or you could grow your plants without soil, in a mixture of sand and vermiculite, if you lined the basket with plastic and made plug holes in it for drainage. The most trouble-free method of watering any hanging basket, by the way, is to take it down last thing at night, leave it in a bucket until morning, then let it drain and hang it up. This soaking should suffice in all but the hottest weather.

If you have planted your basket with bulbs in September then you won't need to bring it in for the winter, though its previous occupant – geraniums, for instance – will need taking indoors. If you are not putting bulbs in, then you can take a chance and leave the basket where it is, covering it completely in a thick plastic bag or even some sacking to keep out the frost. If it is under some sort of cover, then the geraniums should survive, but it's risky so take plenty of cuttings in case your plants don't survive. Or you could simply bring your basket indoors, if you have anywhere suitable to keep it, and with luck things like geraniums will continue to give you colour during the winter if you ensure that they get enough light.

5 Roof Gardens and Balconies

O NCE YOU find yourself with a balcony to garden on, you're definitely one up on the bed-sitter and window box brigade – make it a roof garden and you're really talking in terms of space. But each of these gardens has its own peculiar problems, things you don't think about, perhaps, when you first start to plant.

Take a roof garden for instance – and a lot of people overlook the fact that you can make a garden on almost any roof if you have access to the area around the chimney pots, even if it is only by fixing a series of flowering troughs around the sloping roof top or eaves. One of the biggest problems that the roof gardener has to face is the fact that unless you live in the shadow of a skyscraper your garden is going to be prone to trouble from prevailing winds, especially gales. Plants up there will be very vulnerable and may need sheltering with trellis (and that would have to be well-fixed) or something grown specifically as a windbreak. Another trouble is pollution from city dirt and from neighbours' chimneys; even if you live in a so-called smokeless area your plants may need dusting down and sponging frequently.

Before you even start to plant it's obvious that professional advice is essential to find out exactly what weight your roof will stand. It may *look* solid enough and probably is for you to walk on, but the combined weight of a lot of soil, especially when it is damp, some hefty plants and some concrete troughs may put a strain on it that it was never intended to bear. However, it *is* possible in many cases to strengthen a roof specially, so that it will take that extra load. And if you are staying put for any length of time it is a good financial proposition and will in any case increase the value of your house or flat. If you're leasing the property check that the landlord doesn't mind about your garden plans.

Roof gardens are not normally designed to please the neighbours

Trees, trellis and even a lawn are possible in a roof garden

or give a good show of colour for the street below. They are private places meant for dining out – if you've been wise enough to instal some sort of outdoor cooking equipment like a gas-fired barbecue for instance – and above all for sunbathing (in the nude, if you are lucky enough not to be closely overlooked). So it's obvious that the garden should have some shelter at one end to shield the diners and sunbathers from winds, and somewhere to sit out – and that's where a lawn comes in. To have a lawn on a roof sounds total madness but it isn't, not if you make one from the non-flowering chamomile, *Anthemis nobilis* 'Treneague'. No problems then about lugging a lawn mower up several flights of stairs; this one really doesn't need cutting since it is a prostrate smotherer. It gives you a vivid emerald green lawn of the kind you rarely get with real grass.

Planning a roof garden

Remember that a roof garden is normally an island unto itself – it is probably surrounded by factory chimneys and roofs so it has to be self-sufficient, unless you want to let in a breath-taking view. So it needs framing in some way if you are not to have a slight feeling of giddiness as you walk around it. It may be possible to have avenues of trees edging your garden, provided you grow them in tubs. (It's quite useless to expect to be able to have deep enough soil to plant trees in beds and anyway it would be a dangerous practice as they could damage the roof structure.) If trees are out of the question because of weight, then that is where the climbers come in. Keep things as lightweight as you can; use a wooden trellis, put up professionally if possible, round the edge and let climbers scramble up it – choose the shallower-rooting kind and you can keep them in a flower bed.

Another way to keep weight down, if that is your problem, is to make retaining walls on flower-beds with peat blocks instead of bricks; the saving in time and weight is tremendous. You don't need to cement the blocks together, of course, you can poke little alpine flowers in the cracks and they will positively thrive, and the peat will look more rural than bricks would do. Another material that is lighter than brick is the breeze-block, but it comes in a rather unattractive grey and really needs covering with smothering plants – though it could be quite effective if you planted tiny silver scrambling plants in the indentation on its side edge, then fill the bed with silvery plants too. Remember though that you can plant as many bright colours as you want for the rather smoky city air tends to cover everything with a greyish look.

Coping with soil problems

It's obvious that all soil has got to be laboriously carried up to the roof. If you're lucky you may be able to rig up a block and tackle or something to lift it up straight from the street but otherwise it's more than likely that it will be the stairs or nothing. Soil is something that you shouldn't skimp on; since you're going to so much trouble to get it there, it should be the best that you can afford and weed-free, too, for it's adding insult to injury to inadvertently cart a lot of weed seeds up with you. Loam and leafmould both make ideal media for growing roof-top plants in, but there's no reason why you shouldn't switch about since you've got to get all your soil from somewhere; you could have some plants in beds of acid soil and others in a chalky soil, so that you can have the best of both worlds as far as choice of plants is concerned.

For a perfect soil balance and freedom from weeds at the start, you could buy bags of John Innes No 3 – you might even be able to tip the delivery man to carry them up for you – but to use them to fill a whole roof garden would be extremely expensive, so it's best to cultivate a gardening friend who has some good fibrous loam to spare. Whatever the soil, you can eke it out and lighten it a little with the help of some peat.

How to get it up the stairs? I've found a plastic dustbin of a fairly small size the best container. Otherwise, if you can lay your hands on really tough paper bags – the kind used for storing rubbish – they are fine and unlikely to tear if they are only used once or twice. But never use a sack or a cardboard box – it will certainly spill some of the contents and trying to get damp soil off a pale stair carpet is an appalling, backbreaking task.

A roof garden tends to dry out rather more than an ordinary one does, so you've got to have a point for a hose or sprinkler; don't think in terms of carrying buckets up and down stairs or you'll come to hate your garden and everything it stands for. This is where peat is so useful, for if you keep it damp and don't let it dry out into granules, it will hold water nicely without becoming sticky and heavy. If your roof would take the strain, another answer to the watering problem is to instal a waterbutt or container of any sort to catch rain. Although the garden itself will get rained on, the combined heat from above and below – coming down from the sun and up from the house through the roof space – will tend to dry the plants out quicker than normally.

Drainage is another important problem – no roof is going to like holding pools of water on it after heavy rain. If it's flat it should already have some sort of drainage and it's important not to clog this up in any way. If it has no drainage, then you may have to go to the expense of putting it in. You should put broken pieces of pot and stones down first, before adding the soil into containers or beds, to make sure that they drain properly; also, be sure to take any waterproofing you put down on the roof up the side walls as well.

Drainage helps to stop the soil on the roof from becoming sour after a time.

A pool on the roof

What can you plant on a roof garden? Anything that will grow in a tiny yard or on a patio, and that means most shrubs, dwarf trees, creepers and climbers, if you give them something to scramble up. You could also have a small pond; here fibreglass would be a sensible choice because of the enormous weight of a concrete container or a sink. If you didn't want the conventional blue pool, then look out for a huge trough or cistern made in that dark grey fibreglass that looks exactly like lead, or an urn – that way you combine an attractive appearance with light weight.

Don't forget to leave room for a couple of chairs – as I said, the roof garden is a place to relax! Don't forget to fix some lighting for summer nights. Electricity should be easily accessible; otherwise, lots of shops sell attractive oil lamps and outdoor candle holders. But remember in a hot summer they are going to attract all the moths and mosquitos from miles around – as indeed your garden will be a magnet for birds by day – so remember to hang your lamp well away from where you are sitting, whatever you do.

Reflections on the balcony

A balcony can range from a minute space where there is barely room for you to turn round to the conventional kind of place you get outside the bedroom of a brand-new package hotel – room for two chairs and a table. Either way there's a lot that can be done to improve it.

You can stretch its apparent size by using mirrors on each side wall – more about that in Chapter 10 – or by using one of the sheet mirror substitutes now available. You can keep it as uncluttered as possible, if it has a see-through rail in front, by fixing the window boxes and hanging half-baskets firmly on the *outside* of the rail so that you still get the benefit of them but they don't clutter up the balcony itself. Don't forget to fix at least one hanging basket overhead, planted with trailers; it all helps to give a cloak of colour.

Boxes and half-baskets can be fixed on
the outside of a balcony rail

Climbers are essential to soften up stark lines, and morning glory
is a quick-growing one that will roar away once you get it going.
Alternatively if you catch the sun, sunflowers ranged along the walls
or 'black-eyed Susan' daisies (*Rudbeckia hirta*) are a cheap and easy
way of growing your own wall decoration. Don't forget vegetables
such as runner beans – plant runners in May and they will give you
greenery most of the summer and a bonus in food too. For problems
of shade, any of the climbers suitable for a shady or north wall can
be grown on a balcony, so can ferns, fuchsias, begonias and pansies.
Primroses and primulas, too, prefer a shady place and you could
have them in window boxes placed on the floor.

If your balcony is large enough, you could have shelves going
back like steps on either side, overflowing with containers of
plants. Remember a container doesn't have to be anything expensive; an old colander makes an attractive hanging basket if you
paint it and even plastic dustbins in bright colours, turned so that
their handles are at the back, make a very practical way to grow
plants. You can transport them easily and it is perfectly simple to
make holes in the bottom or better still, from the point of view of
transport, round the sides about 1 in from the base. If you want

C

your balcony to look as large and uncluttered as possible, then paint all your containers the same colour – preferably the same as the walls – and stick to a one or two colour planting at the most. You could even have an all-white balcony garden if the actual walls and floor were in bright colours to set off the plants.

Points to remember

Although your balcony may have more light overall than a tiny town garden at ground level, if it has high sides and an overhanging roof then the light may all come from one direction. So, as with a window sill, you should turn and switch round the plants from time to time, to make sure that all get a fair share of the sun. As with a roof garden, you need to watch the weight, and if you are doing anything very ambitious *and* planning to sit out there, it's best to take professional advice. A rickety balcony can still have its flowers, but they are safer put in half-baskets or boxes on the actual wall of the house, on either side or indoors, just inside the door or window that looks out on it.

If you lease your property, check that there is no small print anywhere that says you can't grow things on a balcony – it's highly unlikely but it could just happen. If you have a solid half wall in the front of your balcony, check how much light plants placed inside it will get; you may find that you have to stick to shade lovers. The other alternative of course is to place window boxes actually along the top of the wall, but it's vital in this case to make sure they are fixed adequately. *You* may be careful not to lean on them and cause them to topple, but you can't always be sure about the casual visitor who steps out to admire the view.

A miniature greenhouse

Bulbs are a blessing for balconies, especially if they are sheltered, since you can force them in a dark cupboard and then bring them out early, long before they are blooming at ground level, and have a show of colour in front of you. Herbs will of course grow well here too and help out not only with greenery in general but with the soft silver grey of sage and the attractive iridescent blue-green of rue.

66

You could also make a miniature greenhouse on a balcony by glassing over one side wall, the one that gets most sun, or you might be able to buy something like a discarded shop show-case that would do the trick. Someone I know had a rather unattractive glass-fronted Edwardian bookcase. She discarded the bottom half, painted the woodwork of the top white and made herself an attractive greenhouse for delicate plants, with doors that opened easily. It's an idea for a way to grow more delicate things; you could also use a bell jar or the domed glass that had once decorated a stuffed owl, to bring on plants.

Hydroponics – a way of growing plants without the normal soil but in a moist aggregate, some sand or vermiculite, is a clean and tidy way of growing things on a balcony. It may be lighter, too, than using soil if you're worried about weight. I've never actually weighed water and soil by volume, but it would be interesting to see if you can save a pound or two that way – more about hydroponics in Chapter 9.

Unusual plants for the balcony

Conventional balcony flowers are the same ones that you would find in hanging baskets and window boxes but there are other things you can raise too. You could for instance have a display of cacti which would certainly cut down your watering problems, or have a stone sink or two with dwarf alpines in. A balcony makes an ideal show place for bonsai, especially if they are evergreen, for it is a great mistake to have a one-season garden; you'll find that you need that greenery and colour more almost in the winter time than you do in summer. If you decide to grow something that likes an exotic, rather humid atmosphere – and many plants that we think of normally as house plants, such as *Monstera*, can be grown safely out on a balcony during the summer months – hose the floor and walls of the balcony down if it looks like being a hot day and the plants will benefit from the steam heat that it generates.

Some plants that flower arrangers grow to bring indoors and dry can be kept on a balcony after they have died off, including statice, honesty and even gourds. Leave them to dry naturally in the sun, then, when they are ready, spray them *in situ* with paint (protecting the wall of course by Sellotaping newspaper over it first) and let them stay there through the winter to give interest and colour. This idea only works on a balcony that is protected from the elements – otherwise the plants will simply rot away in the rain.

6 Finding Room for Vegetables

I T COULD be said, I suppose, that trying to grow vegetables on a balcony or in a tiny back yard is flying in the face of Nature and that it would be better to put your name down for an allotment instead if you live in town. But there's a great something-for-nothing satisfaction to be got from coaxing vegetables out of a confined space or fitting them in among flowers. There is something very satisfying, too, about leaning out of your window and picking tomatoes from plants growing in a box outside or snipping off some herbs to add to an omelette. And there's no doubt either that with all the extra attention that they get, singled out as they are to grow in tubs or pots or a special bed, your vegetables will certainly reward you with high quality to make up for any lack in quantity.

Some things are clearly wasteful to grow – cabbages and potatoes for instance. Yet every spring I plonk a few seed potatoes on the surface of the soil in a tub or two that happens to be unoccupied at the time, cover them with black polythene then, when they sprout, cut holes for the shoots as they poke through. Several weeks later I have my own delicious new potatoes – the ones in the shops never taste quite the same – without having to grovel in the ground for them or having to bank them up. As it happens I don't use English seed potatoes. A couple of years ago in France, when we were catering for ourselves on holiday, I bought some potatoes in the local market that were so tasty, so totally unlike anything I've ever found here, that I brought some home with me to plant. And so every year I keep a few back from the crop to perpetuate the line. It does illustrate one important point, that if space is very limited it's best to go for the really top quality things – and for the unusual, if you can.

Unusual salad plants

While cabbage lettuces would be rather a nonsense to grow, something like the 'salad bowl' lettuce in a pot is worthwhile (you can cut out the centre and new leaves will form). 'Webbs Wonderful', a round lettuce with a nice crisp heart, works well too; so does 'Little Gem', a dwarf Cos that is all heart with few coarse outside leaves. Other things for salad days that take well to window boxes or pots are corn salad (better grown in a pot than in the ground for it keeps the leaves clean), Chinese cabbage, an elongated Cos with pale leaves, or Rocket which gives an unusual flavour to a salad. You can get them all easily in seed form though probably not as small plants. All these salad things will give you some attractive greenery while they grow and the advantage of picking something absolutely crisp and fresh. If you have a flower bed in the garden they can fit into that without any trouble.

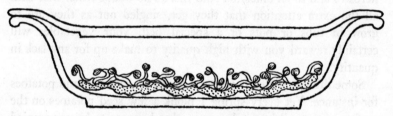

Growing Mung beans in a pie-dish

Moving indoors, the flat dweller who has a penchant for Chinese food or is on a 'wholefoods' kick will find the Chinese Mung bean, or bean sprouts as they're called when grown, ridiculously easy to grow in a cupboard or a drawer. You simply soak a handful over-night in warm water, then scatter them on a damp piece of flannel or old clean sheet – any sort of cloth, J-cloths are fine – spread in the bottom of a pie-dish. Cover them carefully with a plate to exclude all the light, put them away somewhere and a week later your bean sprouts are ready. You can eat them raw in a salad or mixed up with peppers and rice, when they give a crisp, crunchy taste or you can boil or stir-fry them for two minutes, no more, to accompany barbecued spare ribs or any other form of Chinese food. I make a practice of getting a plateful going every Friday so I know I'll have a supply to draw on the following weekend. Sutton's Seeds stock them or you can buy them loose in a Chinese provision shop.

It's nonsense to think that you can't grow even quite bulky vegetables in pots – those huge straight-sided carrots and parsnips you see at horticultural shows have, more often than not, been brought up that way so that they can be watched carefully and made sure they're ramrod-straight. But instead of carrots and parsnips you should go for salsify and scorzonera, two root vegetables that it is almost impossible to find now in the shops. In both cases the roots need boiling (those of scorzonera are black-skinned) then slicing and frying in butter.

Pink runner beans

Some vegetables are so decorative that it is well worthwhile planting them for their appearance alone. Runner beans are a case in point since they don't have to be trained up sticks. They can be left to ramble over netting, a small shrub, anything, or even to hang down from a window box – provided you can get at the crop to pick it. Indeed at one time the runner bean was grown in this country for its looks rather than as a food. If you utilise a wall for it you're saving valuable garden space or it can be grown quite compactly on a cylinder of wire netting which will often stay put rather better than sticks.

Don't forget the dwarf golden butter bean that can be stowed away between flowers or another dwarf which is stringless called 'Tiny Green Snap'. I've had tremendous success with a new runner bean this year called 'Sunset', using it partly for decoration, for instead of the usual scarlet it has flowers of a salmon pink shade which is most un-bean-like, and it crops magnificently. I put eight seeds in each of four Versailles tubs, reducing them down to four if they all germinated, and trained them up tripods of bamboo with a few nasturtiums popped in between them to train over the sides. The result has made a marvellous screen and I have had several good helpings of delicious crisp young beans that didn't need stringing, with plenty more to come. I made sure, of course, that the soil contained plenty of food, for beans are greedy feeders. I dug in

Runner beans grown in Versailles tubs
make an effective screen

plenty of compost from a local mushroom farm, which is very cheap if you take it away, and put lots of small stones for drainage in the bottom of the tubs.

In a window box nearby I mixed sweet peas as trailers with 'Gullivert', the real French petit pois pea. The sweet pea I planted was the new wine-coloured one called 'Beaujolais' which made a good foil for the white flowers of the other pea. Also worth growing in a window box are the sugar pea, 'Carouby de Maussane' for 'mangetout' pods. Of the standard peas, 'Little Marvel' stands up well to town conditions and gives large quantities of small, very sweet peas.

Cucumbers and marrows

There are all sorts of vegetable that can be grown on a balcony but anything that climbs is naturally more decorative and space saving. Start cucumbers off in soil blocks or pots in April, keep them on the window sill indoors (they need plenty of water) then move them out in mid-May. Quite apart from the classic ridge cucumber there is the apple cucumber which is said to be less indigestible than the others and a strange-looking one, the serpent cucumber, which produces fruit that curls round in a spiral. It's got a taste that is slightly different from the others with a faint sweetness about it. Another thing that is easy to grow coming from the same family is the gherkin – 'Venlo Pickling' is the most popular kind. Cucumbers need plenty of food and can be left simply to trail or trained up netting on the side of a balcony wall.

Marrows are very easy to grow – it pays here to buy a ready-started plant, I think, than take up space with seeds. You can get it in a bush variety if you don't want it to ramble too much (one I have at the moment has made growth about 10 ft long). I never let my marrows get much beyond a stage halfway between a courgette and a big 'un. I find then I have quite enough vegetable for two and I don't have to scoop out the pips. You can however get a courgette marrow, an F^1 hybrid which fruits early and goes on producing tiny marrows for you over a long period; the more you pick the more it grows. People do all sorts of strange things with marrows, like drip-feeding them with sugar to make them grow huge. I think the time is better spent in trying several different varieties like the custard bush, for instance, which looks very decorative on a balcony – it's flat and yellow and has frilled edges.

Another climber that takes to the balcony well is the *capsicum* or sweet pepper which ripens remarkably well out of doors. You could even try raising a Canteloupe melon too if you have a sunny sheltered wall, and put some clear plastic in front of it in the spring and early summer. Never let the clear plastic come in contact with

C*

leaves or flowers (and this goes for all plants) or it will almost certainly scorch them in the sunlight.

Herbs in odd corners

Of all the plants that take to window sills and balconies, herbs are by far the most practical proposition, since you're much more likely to be adventurous with them in cooking if all you have to do is lean out and snip off a few fronds of dill, or some tips of marjoram with a pair of scissors. I've even seen parsley grown in a window box; it takes so long to germinate that it is best to put the seeds in tiny fibre pots or soil blocks and put them out when they germinate. Growing herbs in this way in pots is the easiest way to confine those happy wanderers, mint and horseradish. Kept in a large pot and constantly cut, mint won't go straggly and unpleasant. One cook I know has a large pot on the window sill right in front of the kitchen sink in which she has

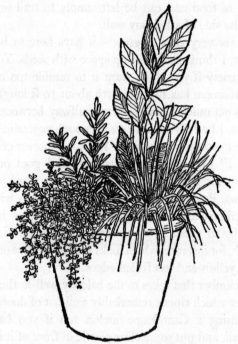

Grow a *bouquet garni* on your window sill

planted a *bouquet garni* of herbs together. The pot has been painted white and with the lush green of the herbs the effect is stunning.

Another way of dealing with herbs if you have a small back yard is to plant some of them between flagstones. Thyme takes very well to being treated this way, so do chamomile, marjoram, mint and chives. They also give off delightful aromatic scents as you tread them underfoot. A good collection of herbs to start with are sage and rosemary in tubs, dill and cardamom sown in window boxes as

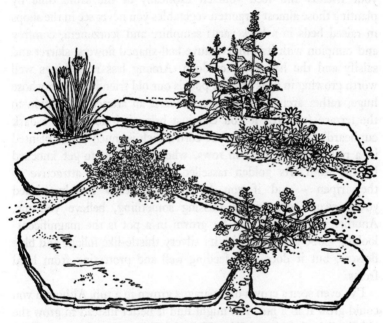

Herbs can be grown between flagstones

annuals, then fennel, thyme and mint in pots. Chives are useful to have on hand in this way, while if you have room for it, buy the perennial form of fennel and put it in a flower-bed or tub where it can establish its long tap root and get going. As with most herbs, fennel loses its aromatic properties if allowed to flower, but the seeds can be used as well as the leaves and can be kept over winter. The annual form of fennel which comes from Italy is a beast to grow, but can be kept in pots – mine keeps dying on me.

Herbs are on the whole moisture lovers, with the exception of rosemary and sage. Plant or sow them in the spring and if you are sowing seed, mark the place carefully – it's very confusing when the first shoots appear and you can't remember whether its chervil or borage or basil that you've put there.

Exotic vegetables

Be adventurous over your vegetable growing. You can confound your friends and feed yourself exotically at the same time by planting those almost forgotten vegetables you never see in the shops in raised beds in a back yard: samphire and scorzonera, comfrey and rampion with its pinky-mauve bell-shaped flowers, skirret and salsify and the handsome cardoon. Among less rare things well worth growing in tubs or large pots is our old friend rhubarb whose huge, rather architectural leaves make it an attractive addition to the terrace (to force it you can just bring it indoors into a dark cupboard). Then there's sweet corn which is much better planted in a round cluster than in rows, when it's liable to get knocked by the wind. Its golden tasselled cobs look very attractive as they ripen – and if you haven't had really freshly picked young sweet corn you're missing something, believe you me. Another plant which can be grown in a pot is the magnificent-looking globe artichoke with its silvery thistle-like foliage and blue flowers, but it does need feeding well and protecting from hard frosts.

I've even seen a crown of asparagus grown in a tub. Although you could grow it in a pot, you might find it better instead to grow the old English plant 'good King Henry' (*Chenopodium bonus-henricus*) whose fleshy shoots taste very much like asparagus and whose leaves can be eaten raw in a salad or cooked like spinach. The tree onion is a space-saving curiosity for a small back yard where ordinary onions would take up too much space. You could also grow it against the wall of a balcony. It is, strangely enough, related to the lily family and its official name is *Allium cepa aggregatum*. Instead of making bulbs at the base it produces them up in the air which certainly makes picking an easy matter. It's a perennial and you don't get a crop until the second year; from then on the quantity improves annually. Beg some bulbets if you can for planting rather than seeds for it cuts down growing time.

Some unfamiliar tomatoes

It's a waste of time in a mini-garden growing conventional tomatoes which tend to come into fruit just when they are at their cheapest in the shops, although they certainly taste much better. But if you buy baby plants early, bring them on indoors, then stand them against a sunny brick wall, you can beat the greengrocer yet. Much more interesting in my view are the special varieties you just can't buy over the counter. There's 'Golden Jubilee', for instance, a delicious golden yellow fruit that tastes very slightly different from the ordinary tomato and looks like sliced yellow pepper when put in a salad. Then there's the Italian plum which grows in a pendulous shape and in a smallish size, the grape tomato which is smaller still and the smallest one of all, 'Tiny Tim', which has fruits the size of cherries and won't grow more than 1 ft. 6 in. high. Another variety still, a new one, is 'Tigrella' which has curious red and yellow stripes all over the fruit. I have it growing in a window box mixed with geraniums and bedding begonias and it fits in very well. For tomato production on a more intensive scale you can't really beat the 'Amateur' which doesn't need staking. It used to be my great stand-by when I lived on a sailing barge. I grew it in boxes on the decks and it had a bushy look about it and plenty of fruit.

Strawberries in pots

Soft fruit is difficult to grow in a very small garden; raspberries, gooseberries and currants take up so much room. But the alpine strawberry with the kind of flavour you'd forgotten ever existed is not so woody as fraise des bois but it is almost as small. Alpine strawberries take very well to being grown in a barrel, in separate pots or indeed on a raised flower-bed. The nicest way to tackle them, in my opinion, is to buy a special terra cotta pot which is almost like a strawberry barrel in miniature, but of a more elegant shape. Plant it with good soil with plenty of liquid feed and fertilizer, then put the small plants in, having either raised them from seed or bought them in young. I have several pots each with seven strawberry plants packed into them and the crop I have had from them is simply amazing. The pots look so decorative that you can bring them on to a dining table, as they are, and pick your own strawberries from there.

It's a great temptation, if you are growing vegetables in earnest, to give them a good feed of manure if a dray horse happens to pass

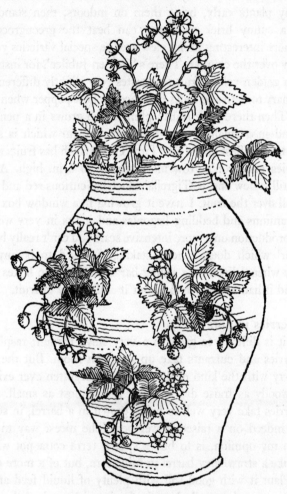

It's worth buying a special pot for
growing alpine strawberries

by. But in a very confined space, especially on a hot night, manure spread around on beds and troughs can give your garden an unpleasant stable-like smell. It's far better to shovel it on to a piece of old sheet and tie it into a bag and suspend it in a bucket. Used as a liquid feed in this way its smell is less obtrusive.

7 Small-scale Water Gardens

I HAVE A friend who was so thrown by the minute size of the garden that went with her London house that she simply turned the whole thing into a swimming pool. Though this action may seem rather drastic – and expensive – for the rest of us to contemplate, there's no doubt that water does give an added dimension to a very small back yard. There's no need, incidentally, to dig a hole in order to have a pool; in small surroundings it often looks better on a raised-up level. Water doesn't have to be confined to the garden, either; it's perfectly feasible to have a mini-pool on a balcony or roof garden.

At its most basic, you can make quite a respectable little pool out of an old stone sink with a few decorative pebbles arranged on the bottom, placed on a patio as a water-trough; there's no need to bury it in the ground. If it is deep enough it could even support a water lily or two.

There are lots of advantages in having a pool in a very small garden. For one thing, it is bound to be so near to the house that laying on water or electricity should be no problem, and for another, you will certainly be able to appreciate it from your window. You *could* have a small pond dug out and lined with concrete in the corner of a back yard, but that's really going to an unnecessary expense unless, for instance, you're having a patio built, in which case it's an easy matter to build it in. A tiny pool makes an attractive addition to a chequerboard garden too, adding to the patchwork of pebbles, chamomile and flowers.

Using plastic sheeting
If you can't get the square shape you want ready made in fibreglass form, it's a relatively easy matter to dig out a hole, making the sides go in steps rather than straight up (or you'll get little landslides of earth into the water from time to time), then line the hole with the

The chequerboard garden can include a tiny pool

heaviest duty polythene you can get, preferably in black which makes the pool look deeper.

How to calculate what you'll need? Just measure the length and width of the hole, and add *twice* the depth of the hole to each measurement. In other words if your pool is to be 2 ft by 3 ft and 1 ft deep, you add 1 ft twice to the 2 ft, and 1 ft twice again to the 3 ft – totalling 20 sq ft in all, or 5 ft by 4 ft Never, *never* use just any old piece of plastic for a pool, it's a waste of time and effort for it will puncture almost before you've had a chance to fill it.

To 'set' the polythene in place, lay it out carefully over the hole (it's much easier to do this in warm weather when it is more pliable) and put a little soil in the bottom and on the steps at the side, then fill it gently with a hose to avoid disturbing the soil. Once it's full, smooth any surplus flat over the surrounding soil and cover it as quickly as you can with decorative pieces of paving stone or brick.

Installing a fibreglass pool

A rather more permanent proposition is a ready-made fibreglass pool – unfortunately they seem to come mainly in variations of the kidney shape and in a Mediterranean blue that looks rather out of place in Britain. But once you've covered its bath-tub-like rim with turf or paving stones it blends in remarkably well. It looks particularly pretty surrounded by a chamomile lawn with one or two spiky plants such as an iris, for instance, reflected in the water. Remember, by the way, that if you're putting your pool in a flower-bed, there's no need really to dig a hole for it. You can make the smallest indentation, plonk the pool shape on top, then bank up the earth round and plant it with ground-covering plants; alternatively you can make a little wall of peat blocks, filling in any corners that don't fit with loose earth.

Pools for the balcony or roof

Pools on roof gardens can be treated this way, but when it comes to a balcony something more self-contained is needed, and this is where the trough or an urn comes in. A garden urn on a small pedestal makes a perfect pool; you can even grow a water lily in it, and if it's large enough you could also add a fountain. Alternatively a water-tight trough at one end of a balcony can be lit up at night, and a fountain can easily be fixed on the wall to shower into it.

One word about water on balconies and roofs – remember the neighbours. What seems like a cooling waterfall to you, cleverly contrived with plastic and a pump, on a windy day could drench your next-door-neighbour on *her* balcony adjoining yours or spray the people below. And if you've ever walked past a building that is being washed you'll know what *that* feels like! Even so, it pays to have some sort of movement in your water garden wherever it is, if you live in city conditions, otherwise dust and dirt will make an unattractive film on the surface of the water in no time at all. A submersible pump is the cheapest and easiest way of installing a fountain in a small pool – indeed you can get them in such small sizes that they can even be used as part of a table decoration. They're relatively silent in operation too, but you do have the 'works' showing under the water; the best way to hide them is with a handful of pebbles. The jets, incidentally, can be adjusted to give a high spray or something more moderate if you have fish and/or water lilies in your pool.

**A garden urn makes a perfect pool for a balcony; a flimsy tub
can be made watertight by placing a plastic bucket inside**

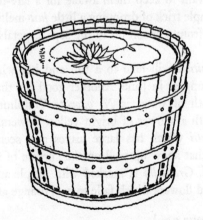

Lilies to grow in bowls and tubs

Water lilies may sound an exotic proposition for a small garden or a balcony but they're surprisingly agreeable and easy to grow; some come in miniature versions that could be grown easily on a window sill. *Nymphaea pygmaea alba* (*Nymphaea* is the generic name) is the smallest water lily of all; it has tiny, white, scented flowers just 2 in across; you can root it in a salad bowl and it will flourish in water 6 in deep or less. Another good window sill water lily is *Nymphaea pygmaea* 'Helvola' which has tiny yellow flowers and will grow in a pudding basin.

If you're thinking in terms of tubs, the choice is surprisingly large – and your tub, incidentally, could be one of those attractive but rather flimsy wooden ones that won't hold water but are cheap to buy, with a large plastic bucket placed strategically inside, doing all the real work. Best for the really small tub or urn are the three *N.* × *laydekeri* lilies: 'Fulgens' which gives a generous profusion of rich red flowers, 'Lilacea' which is more delicate with pink and white flowers that change to deep crimson and 'Purpurata' which is a darker crimson still. The interesting thing about water lilies, incidentally, is the way that they change colour as they develop. They open in the morning, and start to close up by the afternoon again; if you want to keep them awake for a late-night party, you can use the simple trick of dropping a little *just*-melted wax, or even ordinary lard, from a spoon on to the sepals, petals and stamen at the base.

Nymphaea nitida will take to a tub and has white cup-shaped flowers which appear in June. Another good lily that doesn't need too much depth of water is *N. odorata* 'Sulphurea' which will reward you with a shower of bright yellow flowers. For fragrance pick *N. Froebelii* which has large leaves and scented flowers of dark crimson that show up well on the surface of still water. For leaf interest *N. Graziella* is marked with purple and has reddish-bronze coloured flowers which fade to cool orange afterwards.

Flowers for your pool

Coming on to small pool size, the hybrid lily 'Aurora' needs only about 9 in of water, has deep yellow flowers which darken to orange, and dark red, mottled leaves that give it a tropical appearance. The flowers of *N.* × *robinsonii* are long-stayers and an attractive yellow just tinged with red. This plant needs about 12 in. of water. 'Solfatare', another one to try, is more delicate in its colouring with yellow flowers tipped with pink. A more flamboyant choice would be 'Firecrest', an American hybrid which has bright pink, scented flowers.

For the pool proper a good hardy lily to plant is 'James Brydon' which has rich deep red flowers which float on the water in profusion, or there's 'Ellisiana' which needs about 12 in of water and has deep bright vermilion flowers with clashing orange stamens. All water-lilies should be given the minimum of water depth they need if you are to encourage them to flower.

With all this profusion of flowers to choose from – and I've only mentioned some of the best-known ones – you could give over your entire terrace, backyard or balcony to them. It would solve your watering problems because all you would need to do is to top up the containers occasionally. They're certainly an idea for the flat or house owner who is away frequently on business and has difficulty finding a plant or window-box sitter to come in and water the plants.

Planting your lily

Water lilies should be planted in May or June and should always be bought from a specialist grower; there are plenty dotted about throughout the country. If the pool has only just been installed or the tub only just bought, fill it with water and leave it for a day or so so that the temperature can rise from the rather icy state in which it came out of the tap. If you're planting in a pond, then shovel about 4 in-depth of good soil in the bottom (don't use leafmould or it will turn sour) and add a little crushed charcoal to keep it sweet. It will take two or three days for the water to warm up and the soil to settle and then you are ready to put in the lily. If you can lay your hand on a little turf, put this on top of the soil; it will keep it from becoming stirred up and turning the pond muddy and make a good, sound base for the lily roots to penetrate. Lower the water lily tuber very carefully into the water, anchor the roots down with a few pebbles or stones and then check that the crown of the lily is only

Anchor the lily's roots with a few stones and adjust the water level if
necessary

just covered by water; if it is way underneath, then bale some water
out of the pond. Lilies with rhizome-like roots which resemble an
iris should have them placed flat on the earth in the pond; other
tubers should be stood upright, like bulbs.

You can plant small water lilies in tubs by the method that I've
described, but it's sometimes more convenient to give them their
own root container. Those small plastic mesh cartons in which
greengrocers sometimes sell soft fruit are fine for the purpose.
Treat them to some heavy compost mixed with a little bonemeal to
give the plant a good send-off. If you want to keep the water
level higher in the tub than the lily can stand, you can place the
container on a brick or something similar at first, then remove it, and
lower the carton in place a few weeks later. This gives the plant a
chance to put out new leaves for, strange to say, a water lily can be
drowned.

Achieving a balanced ecology
To keep a pool sweet without a filter, or without changing the water
– a time-consuming business – it's a good idea to provide some pond
life. Fish – goldfish at any rate – need a minimum depth of water of
18 in, better still 2 ft, and to calculate how many you need to stock

your pond work on the assumption that a goldfish needs a minimum of two square feet of water to itself. Put any pond plants, including water lilies, in first, before you stock with fish. Give them a chance to establish themselves before adding livestock. Don't forget to add some feeding and oxygenating plants like the water violet, *Hottonia palustris* which blooms in early summer and has pretty mauve flowers, and *Azolla caroliniana* which is a miniature mossy plant that floats on the surface. Another good oxygenator is *Callitriche autumnalis* because it works all year round and the fish like to eat its leaves. These plants have a useful side effect in that they keep a pond clean and keep down the algae which can produce an unpleasant green slime on the surface. So even if you are not stocking with fish, it's a good idea, if the pond is any size at all, to include a few oxygenators as well as lilies. If you are going in for fish, by the way, you will need to break the ice on your pool in winter.

Neighbourhood cats can be a menace where fish are concerned. If the surface of the pond is dotted with water lilies (but not entirely covered, or the fish won't be able to survive) then this acts as a deterrent, since it takes a very watchful cat to spot them slipping in and out of the stalks down below. The use of wire netting seems a rather unsightly admission of failure. If you're really keen on keeping fish, and the cats are equally keen on trying to catch them, then the only answer is to have a decorative grille made for the surface of the pond, that rests on the side edges and can be lifted off in a minute. Unfortunately this rather rules out the possibility of growing anything more than dwarf water lilies as well.

Plants to partner pools

A water lily in a tub is the star of its own show; just beam a small spotlight on it at night and it's transformed into something quite unreal and quite lovely. But what you plant around a pond matters. It depends whether it has a rather stark architectural setting, as it might well have if it is sunk into the side of a patio (and I say side, for if you put it too near the back door sooner or later, at a party, one guest who has drunk too much is bound to step into it, and emerge shame-faced with one dripping wet leg). Patio pools require starkly simple planting around them – bamboo, palms, even yucca can be put into pots if you haven't a bed to plant them in, and they all look good in a modern setting.

If you've a pool in a corner, you can't really beat the rhododendron as a partner for it, provided you've a bed of acid soil. Its flowers complement the water lily and as an evergreen its leaves stay put all year round, so you don't have the problem you will always have with deciduous trees of leaf-fall into the water. There's a common fallacy that the iris loves a waterlogged soil, perhaps that's why it is found planted near ponds so often. But the dwarf plant *Iris pumila*, for instance, positively hates a waterlogged home – though if your pond is made from fibreglass or lined with plastic there's no reason why the soil surrounding it should be wet. *Iris pumila* is a good choice for a very small pond since it looks pretty reflected in the water, yet it grows only a few inches high. It's amazingly tough, too, and can be left alone without attention. It you want blue flowers, pick *Iris pumila* 'Caerulea', for yellow flowers look for 'Attica'.

It could be that you have unwittingly got damp soil conditions without a pond – lots of town gardens have a dank corner where the soil seems waterlogged and nothing wants to grow. The double marsh marigold, *Caltha palustris* 'Plena' looks happy either by the side of a pool or in a bog-ridden setting. If it is shady too, then pick *Ranunculus aquatilis* instead. Hardy ferns like moisture, so remember to add them to your list.

In a really waterlogged corner the lady's slipper orchid will positively thrive. In fact there are a number of spotted orchids (some of them, like *Cypripedium reginae* are American in origin) which like nothing better than to lurk in a shady north corner and give you plenty of just cause for one-upmanship when a visitor enquires about them.

8 Trees for the Tiny Garden

TREES HAVE a splendid way of furnishing a small garden or a terrace and giving it a focal point. But even if you have a minute back yard, a balcony, a roof garden or even a window box, you don't have to rule them out of the scheme of things; there are plenty of small varieties that fit.

When it comes to planting on a small scale, fortunately there are dwarf varieties of all the popular trees that can be cleverly used to make an area seem larger than it really is. For instance, if we see a conifer in a tiny garden which appears to be in scale with its surroundings, we tend to think of the garden as being larger than it is rather than of the tree being a dwarf. So a tree can be used to give an illusion of greater space. Don't forget you can use trees, too, as a screen from your neighbours; they can be grown in pots on balconies for this purpose. And you can now buy them already grown to a respectable size in a container which gives you a head start with your landscaping plans.

Many people are afraid of planting trees in a yard or a patio for fear that the roots will run riot and undermine the foundations and rip up the concrete. This is nonsense – pick the right variety and you've nothing to worry about. And if you have a particular yen for something with wandering roots, there's no problem about confining them and keeping the tree down to scale at the same time. The enthusiast who plants a key of the common sycamore right outside his back door *is* asking for trouble though, unless he puts it in a pot.

They need looking after
Trees are remarkably good-tempered once established but they will need watering frequently at first when the roots are settling in and trying, at the same time, to supply the leaves with nourishment. And remember that though you would never dream of watering a tree in a

89

garden, if it is on a terrace or in a tub it needs an eye kept on it in times of drought; evergreen or not, it will soon start to shed its leaves and could eventually die. Another point to watch in city conditions: evergreens particularly become affected by pollution if they are not given a wash and brush up from time to time. If the leaves look dusty and covered with grime, go over them with a damp sponge – don't forget the stems too – and you will be repaid by fresh growth and a perkier look about the tree.

It goes without saying that if you are planting a roof garden, any trees that you use to furnish it – and here you can get up to quite good heights as you've no restriction on space, though bear in mind the effect of high winds – must be confined to tubs or troughs. No-one wants to wake up and see a *thing* growing down through the ceiling from above but this could happen for roots have a habit of literally taking root through anything at all, even roofing felt and lath and plaster. Another practical point to watch is that messy trees, those with catkins, berries or lots of leaves to shed can be tiresome on a patio, over a pond or, indeed, on a balcony since you are constantly sweeping up. But sometimes it's well worth it for the pleasure that they give.

Evergreens for value

For a bare patio or a bleak back yard, there's no doubt that evergreens offer you the best value for money in terms of greenery all year round and it's a pleasure, especially in midwinter, to look out and see them there, whereas bare branches on a bare terrace tend to underline the fact that it's cold outside. I'm not mad about that ubiquitous evergreen Lawson cypress which we usually see used as a quick-growing hedge. But there's no doubt that it takes on an altogether different air when used by itself in a tiny town garden. It's cheap to buy, neat in its habits and it doesn't shed leaves, of course; stood in a corner or set apart by itself, it gives a small plot an Italian air. I prefer the pyramid shaped dark blue-green version *Chamaecyparis lawsoniana* 'Allumii' but there are so many others. There's a weeping version, for instance, *C.l.* 'Bowleri' or one tinged with white, *C.l.* 'Argenteovariegata' or, if you'd like something light and feathery in a golden shade, there is *C.l.* 'Hillieri'.

I suppose you could call the rhododendron a giant shrub rather than a tree, but there's no doubt it is a marvellous all-year-round choice for a back yard. It has to have an acid soil to do well – give it something chalky and it will sulk and turn yellow. But there are ways of coping with this. I live in a very chalky area and have two flourishing rhododendrons in my tiny back yard. One is planted in a special raised bed filled with a mixture of acid soil and some peat. The other is in a tub of chalky soil that has been dosed with Sequestrene. Its leaves were yellow when we first moved here, but are now a nice glossy green. I watch them like a hawk and at the first sign of turning give them some more iron tonic. Rhododendrons have the great advantage that they are shallow rooting so they will fit into a raised bed or reasonable-sized tub quite happily and they don't mind being moved at all. In fact it seems to stimulate their growth, so if you are in a nomadic state at the moment and likely to move your flat, the rhododendron will be happy to move with you. They love shade for they are naturally woodland plants and they do like plenty of water, so they are just the thing for a dank, moist corner.

Trees for colour

For summer and autumn colour the maples and the flowering cherries in Japanese versions are small and give lots of interest in a small plot. Japanese cherries are a godsend for few of them ever reach more than 10 ft high, and although we may not be able to aspire to the great white cherry 'Tai Haku' that you see growing everywhere in Japan, there are several that will suit perfectly. The weeping chrysanthemum cherry, 'Kiku-shidare Sakura', for instance has a shower of pink flowers in spring and will reach about 6 ft high and no more. It will grow happily in a tub too and stays small. If you want to stop it reaching a maximum height, chop off excess root growth by pushing a spade sharply into the ground in a ring around it. Another useful cherry tree to remember is variously known as 'milky way', the 'flagstaff' cherry and the 'maypole' cherry, *Prunus* 'Amanogawa'. It has an erect form of growth like a tall column rather than the open umbrella shape of most cherry trees, and plenty of sugar-pink flowers. It loves chalk, as do most of the *Prunus* family. Against a wall, Snow White (*Prunus* 'Shirotae') has branches that tend to spread slightly horizontally, while for fragrance you can't beat the scented blossoms of *P*. 'Jo-nioi', though it's a strong grower, so be warned. A small round-headed cherry is *P*. 'Fudanzakura' which has a compact round head and flowers intermittently between November and April. It's particularly useful for bringing branches of blossom indoors during the winter time.

The Japanese maples, *Acer japonicum* and *palmatum* offer a wide variety of small trees that turn a gorgeous bronze or crimson in autumn and even with the branches bare they make attractive shapes in the garden. The most brilliant of them all – the leaves look almost as if they are on fire – is *Acer palmatum* 'Heptalobum Osakazuki', while *A. palmatum* 'Heptalobum Rubrum' has the opposite effect – its leaves start off blood-red in spring and pale as the summer goes on.

A magnolia is a happy thought in any soil that is acid or even clay-like – the only one that can stand chalk is *M. kobus*. My favourite for the tiny garden is *M. stellata* which has starry flowers and can be stopped at about 10–11 feet and allowed to become bushy. All magnolias need shelter from prevailing winds and take time to come into flower but the wait is well worthwhile. For a good all-rounder in a small garden, *M. wilsonii* has slender leaves, will thrive in partial shade and keeps itself within bounds.

Trees for town conditions

The locust tree, the false acacia *Robinia pseudoacacia*, takes well to town conditions, has pretty white flowers and makes the dustiest back yard look verdant and green – try growing one as a standard. Don't imagine, incidentally, that you will be able to plant anything more than a handful of bulbs under most town trees. They're going to grab anything that is going in the way of minerals and nourishment from the soil. The mountain ash, *Sorbus scopulina*, is more genteel however, and is prepared to share a bed with all-comers. If the soil is already poor then you can't beat a fig tree which thrives in light, dryish earth and not too much nourishment. Having said that, I'm convinced that a fig does need feeding in its first years while it is getting established. We had one that lingered on in a rather sickly way for five years or more, scarcely showing any sign

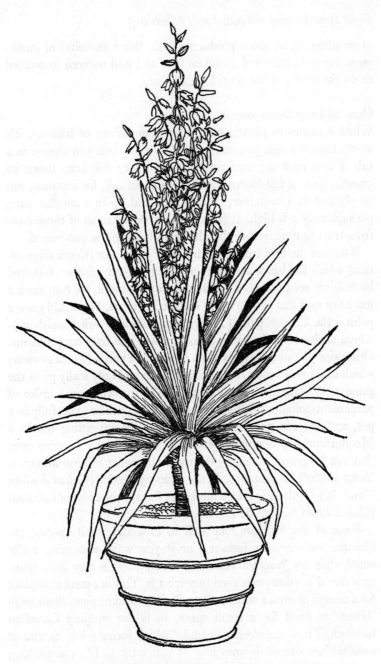

The palm-like *Yucca gloriosa* grows well in a pot

of progressing, let alone producing fruit. But a shovelful of mushroom compost scattered round its base and well watered in seemed to do the trick – it has roared ahead since.

How to keep them small

When it comes to planning trees for your terrace or balcony, it's worth knowing that you can grow almost any tree you choose in a tub if you want to; confining it in that way will keep down its growth. Even a full-blown forest tree like an oak, for instance, can be planted in a container, when it will end up in a smaller state, perhaps only 5 ft high. It pays to cut back the roots of these trees from time to time, rather than let them become too pot-bound.

What are the best trees for tubs? The Judas tree (*Cercis siliquastrum*) which has branches smothered in pinky-blue flowers followed by brilliant seed pods is a useful subject for a small, tall tub, since it has a tap root that can be easily confined to a pot. You could grow a palm – the Chusan palm (*Trachycarpus fortunei*) will flourish anywhere sheltered and as it is a slow grower you have no problems. Otherwise you could always cheat and plant a yucca (*Yucca gloriosa*) which looks very much like a stunted palm and only really gives the game away when it blooms occasionally, throwing up a spike of parchment-coloured, bell-shaped flowers. It works wonderfully in a pot, and you can persuade yourself that you are sitting out in a Mediterranean setting with a yucca around. There are so many trees that can be grown in tubs – the mountain cedar (*Cedrus atlantica*, 'Atlas Cedar') for instance, or the weeping deodar (*Cedrus deodara* 'Pendula'). Or there is even a miniature form of the cedar of Lebanon (*Cedrus libani* 'Comte de Dijon').

Some of the junipers take well to tubs and small spaces; the Chinese varieties, for instance, or if you want something really small, then try *Juniperus communis* 'Compressa', a tiny little blue-grey tree that takes years even to reach 1 ft. This is a good candidate for a trough or even a window box. The alpine knee pine, *Pinus mugo* 'Gnom' is good for a small space, so is the weeping Canadian hemlock, *Tsuga canadensis* 'Pendula' which forms a low mound of overlapping, drooping branches. If you want to plant something near a pond or in a tub, the creeping willow *Salix repens* won't reach

Topiary is fun, even if you need to cheat a little

more than 5 ft, if you leave it unchecked, and can be kept down below that. Another tiny willow tree is *Salix hastata* 'Wehrhanhii', which has pretty silvery catkins. Another good poolside tree is the dwarf birch, a miniature silver birch *Betula nana* which grows only about 5 ft high too, and goes a coppery-red colour in the autumn. For a *really* mini willow look out for *Salix helvetica*; it's a truly tiny tree that will go in a tub or even in a flower pot, or a window trough or a rockery and is not likely ever to go above 3 ft in height.

Try topiary
Although it's inclined to look dingy, box is a perfect subject for a little topiary on the terrace. In a rather unexpected place – Bangkok, to be precise – I saw some amusing elephants, dogs and peacocks cut from box and grown in tubs. Constant trimming will give you the shape that you need and if you want to achieve something

tricky, like an elephant's trunk, you can always cheat a little and wire the branch in the right place; once it has formed a dense and compact mass you won't be able to see the works. *Buxus koreana* is the box to look for; it is a useful item to grow in a window box if you haven't much time and want something to help fill it all year round.

Trees on a terrace or patio have to have immediate appeal, you can't really stand back and admire them, and the same thing goes for a balcony too. So this is where small standards come in. A bay tree trained as a standard has almost become a cliché in a town garden, but you can get them too trained in a pyramid. A bay needs trimming in May and again in July and you should sponge the leaves occasionally. It's not really hardy all the year round unless it is in a sheltered place, so it's best to take it indoors when there is danger of a bad winter frost. Fortunately it looks attractive in a dining room but the most practical place for it, of course, is the kitchen. Save the leaves that you prune off in summer, hang them up with clothes pegs on a line to dry, then pack them in polythene when they get crisp and papery – they're a useful thing to give away for Christmas since they cost quite a lot in the shops.

Turning pot plants into trees

It's very easy to turn a plant into a small standard tree or indeed to train a tree that way; it helps if there is very small space for it since it leaves things clear at ground level. A hibiscus, for instance, will make a splendid small standard tree if you cut away all lower branches or shoots, encourage it to grow to the height you want, then train it into a compact ball of twigs at the top. Don't worry if there is no sign of a leaf until early summer by the way, that's how it is with hibiscus. Make sure that you buy a hardy variety, not one intended for a greenhouse, and give it a sheltered wall.

The pomegranate (*Punica granatum*) can be trained into a standard in a pot and although it is unlikely to give you any fruit, it has lush scarlet flowers. Lemon verbena makes a small standard too, though it needs to go indoors in the winter; it's only really suitable if you have a garage, a greenhouse, a spacious sitting room or a friend who will house it for you. What else can you make into a small standard tree? Geraniums (pelagoniums), fuchsias and even

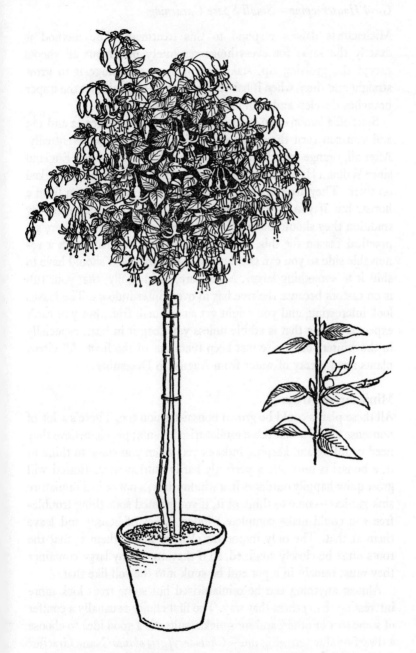

With a little care, a fuchsia can be trained into a small standard tree

D

Michaelmas daisies respond to this treatment. The method is exactly the same for everything: resolutely pinch out all shoots except the growing tip, stake the plant to encourage it to grow straight and then, when it has reached the right height, let the upper branches develop and trim them into a compact ball.

Start off a lemon or an orange pip as described on pages 42 and 123 and you can turn them into decorative standards too, eventually. After all, orange trees have been grown this way in tubs in England since William Harrison, writing in the reign of Elizabeth I, remarked on them. They are relatively expensive to buy ready-grown from a florist, but if you have the patience you can raise your own. By tradition they should be grown in square Versailles tubs – there's a practical reason for this, for the tubs should be made with a removable side so you can get the tree out easily if you should have to shift it to something larger. Make sure, incidentally, that your tub is on castors because the tree has to overwinter indoors. The leaves look interesting, and you might get some small fruit, but you can't expect anything that is edible unless you keep it in heat, especially in the winter; otherwise just keep them out of the frost. All citrus plants need plenty of water from August to December.

Miniaturised trees

All these plants could be grown bonsai-fashion too. There's a lot of nonsense talked about these miniaturised plants; people believe they need coddling and keeping indoors yet, when you come to think of it, a bonsai is normally a perfectly hardy outdoor tree. Bonsai will grow quite happily outdoors in a window box, a pot or in a miniature sink garden – come to think of it, if you wanted something trouble-free you could make complete window boxes of bonsai and leave them at that. The only important element about them is that the roots must be closely confined, so if they are in any large container they must remain in a pot and be sunk into the soil like that.

Almost anything can be miniaturised but some trees look more interesting than others that way. The first choice is usually a conifer of some sort or other, and for quick results it's a good idea to choose a dwarf or slow-growing one – *Chamaecyparis obtusa* 'Nana Gracilis' for instance, the Temple Tree of Japan that grows very slowly indeed, only about half an inch a year. Another good candidate for miniaturising is *Juniperus media* 'Plumosa Aurea', a wide spreading juniper tree that is very slow growing. Then there's the miniature golden holly (*Ilex crenata* 'Golden Gem') which is ideal for a window box or for turning into a bonsai; it has tiny bright golden leaves instead of the usual green. *Picea glauca albertiana* 'Conica' is a very dwarf version of the Christmas tree which makes a good window box or Bonsai candidate. But you can also use oak, spruce, chestnut or sycamore in this way, cedars or even orange and lemon.

Think small and you'll find a new and fascinating spare-time occupation. But you need plenty of patience, too, for it is a matter of years before results really begin to show – that's why I recommend starting with trees that are by their very nature dwarf in size. Start off with a healthy seedling, one that is not too spindly and tall, and put it in a shallow container that restricts its roots, then prune back the top growing tip with scissors. It's the annual root pruning that does it, and makes the tree grow small even down to tiny-sized leaves. If it is an evergreen tree you uncover the roots and tie each one in a knot; if it is deciduous you cut the roots back. Either way, you don't simply allow the plant to become potbound. If you are going into bonsai in any serious way, there are a number of books on the subject giving away such tricks of the trade as wiring the tiny growing branches of the sapling so that they look gnarled and twisted with time.

Give them a good start

A final word on the planting and care of trees in general. Do give them a good start by preparing a really big trough, the larger the better. If the tree is not in a container but covered in sacking or plastic, undo the wrapping and soak the roots thoroughly. Now plant it in the space prepared, disturbing the roots as little as possible; when the tree is on an even keel, undo the roots and spread them out as naturally as possible. Put some compost round the roots and a little soil and dunk the tree up and down, so that there are not large airspaces between the individual roots. Now tread it in well, cover with soil and firm again. If necessary anchor the tree to a post or by means of three or more 'guy' ropes of cord; wrap the tree with a rag or piece of rubber where the cord is tied round it.

It's important to water a tree generously once it has been planted and to remember that anything in unnatural surroundings like a pot or trough will always need an eye kept on it from this point of view. Plant in the winter months whenever possible, even if you're getting a container-grown plant, and your new addition to the garden is bound to flourish and give you great visual pleasure.

9 Plants Without Soil

How would you like a salad ready to pick, growing right beside your refrigerator? Or fresh asparagus thriving on your window sill? They're both possible without using any soil at all, thanks to the science of hydroponics. What puts people off the idea of growing things indoors on a large scale is often the thought of carting all that rather messy worm and beetle ridden earth across the living room carpet or, indeed, if you live in a very self-contained flat, getting it indoors at all. But you can grow almost anything you like using a cleaner, more static medium instead, following the principles of soil-less culture, an idea that was thought up, incidentally, in the beginning of the eighteenth century, but which has only just caught on on a grand scale. Now it's used extensively to grow essential foodstuffs in places like India where the soil is too scanty and impoverished to grow things successfully in some areas.

It may come as a surprise to hear that a plant doesn't *need* soil at all, really, for anything more than support. The vital elements in its life are light and air, water, and essential minerals – which can often be lacking in poor quality earth. As long as it is provided with these basics, it will flourish happily, provided its roots are properly supported. That being so you can – and commercial growers do – produce almost anything you like without soil from flowers to fruit or salads. It's the ideal way of life too, for the unhappy gardener, the type whose plants always pass out on him, since it depends rather more on simple scientific know-how for success than on having green fingers – no more anxious pacing around the *Saintpaulia* in its pot, wondering if it should be watered that day or not, because with hydroponics the moisture problem is made easier. There's no reason, incidentally, why you shouldn't grow plants outdoors this way as well as indoors – it makes for lighter-weight window boxes for one thing. So it's just right for anyone who can't get hold of any soil worth having except by paying for it expensively. What's more, you can grow things anywhere you wish, for if you rig up a fluorescent tube to give light, you can pick the darkest corner of a room for your trough. There's no weeding, naturally, no dirt to get into the lettuce or celery and plants raised this way mature more quickly too.

At its most basic, the growing of bean sprouts or mustard and cress on a flannel is a form of hydroponics; you sprinkle the seed on a supporting base, provide water and darkness and leave them to get on with it. That's fine simply for germination, but if you're growing a full-sized plant in this way it will also need supporting and feeding, and that's what hydroponics is all about.

You replace the earth with a sterile medium that can be one of a number of different things. For the town-dweller the most trouble-free choice is a mixture of coarse sand and vermiculite, which is officially called hydrated magnesium aluminium silicate but which is sold under a number of different names. Other things you can use are coarse sand by itself (though that makes for a heavier container), crushed brick, washed cinders or small pebbles (fine if you've got a beach nearby or a disused home aquarium).

Choosing your containers
First, though, comes your container. You don't need anything as large or as deep for growing plants with the hydroponic method as you would in the conventional way; you don't have to plant seeds so deeply for one thing. Your container does need to be waterproof, up to a point, but more of that later. A shallow seed box that has been lined, an old sink, a bowl or a flower pot are fine – or you could buy something more exotic. If you're planting outdoors you could make yourself a special trough using concrete or bricks and mortar. Whatever kind of container you use, it must be able to retain water satisfactorily but at the same time have drainage holes that can be plugged. If you're using a flower pot, for instance, you should be able to find a cork that will fit in the hole at the bottom.

You can find all sorts of containers specially made for the purpose, but if you are short of cash, a greengrocer's wooden tray is probably the cheapest thing you can lay your hands on. To grow, say, vege-

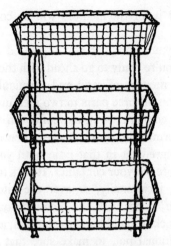

A beanstalk rack lined with plastic floor covering
makes a simple hydroponic unit

tables in it hydroponically, all you need to do is to line it with some
polythene sheeting (pick a good heavyweight quality) fixed in place
by strategically-sited drawing pins. If you wanted to make something more lasting – if, for instance, you were planning to grow
salad crops all the year round – you could make a fibreglass lining
for it. Having lined your box, the next important task is to make
some drainage holes in the side. You'll need two or three on each
long edge, one at either end, placed about half an inch from the
bottom. These can then have plugs of balsa wood, cork, Plasticine,
even chewing gum or surgical tape to keep the water in.

Hydroponic unit for indoors

For a neat, instant, space-saving hydroponic unit in a kitchen I've
used a 'beanstalk' rack with each tray lined with offcuts of a heavy
plastic floor-covering; you could also use heavy-duty plastic or
roofing felt for the job. Another idea is the multi-tiered vegetable
rack which makes a splendid place for growing salads in rotation.
An old kitchen sink makes an ideal container too, though it probably
looks better out of doors rather than in. You simply use the old
drainage plug as it stands, although obviously you can't plant

anything too near it for the medium will be constantly disturbed in that area.

Having found your container and organised adequate drainage holes and plugs, you're ready to go ahead with the growing medium. If you're using a mixture of sand and vermiculite you'll need to stick to a proportion of three parts to two measured by volume, not weight. Take any container – an old coffee tin will do – measure three tinfuls of vermiculite into a bucket, then add two tinfuls of sand. Add each ingredient in that ratio until you have enough to almost, but not quite, fill your container. It pays to do this job out of doors if you can, incidentally, or over the kitchen sink! Before filling your trough or pot with the medium you must first put a layer of rubble, crocks or pebbles at the bottom, as you would when planting a conventional pot, to make sure that there is adequate drainage. This is particularly important with hydroponic gardening to avoid the plant becoming unpleasantly swamped and the roots deprived of air.

First the rubble then, and afterwards the mixed-up medium. Smooth over the surface, make it as level as you can, then water it well and evenly – do this job in the kitchen. Leave the container for about an hour to let the medium take up the moisture and settle, then take out the plugs and let any excess water drain away. At this point I should mention that it's essential to keep your trough or container just raised off the surface of a saucer or a tray, or indeed a special holder to prevent spillage on the floor. If you're using a greengrocer's box, two pieces of battening nailed at either end, or four cotton reels, one in each corner will do the trick. Replace the plugs – don't forget to do that or the result could be rather messy as the weeks go by – and you're all set to plant.

Growing from seed

Seeds germinate anything from three days to a week earlier when grown hydroponically – that's a particularly heartening message in the case of those things like the herb coriander or parsley, another slow grower, which normally seem to take an age to appear. If the seed is large enough, or if you've bought it in pelleted form, then sowing is simple; you just put them in holes made in the medium by a knitting needle or a pencil point, cover them up and leave them. If it's very fine seed, like lettuce for instance, you need to sprinkle it on the surface, then cover it with a layer of sand. Either way, don't bury your seeds as deeply as you would in the usual way – half an inch is the maximum – you need just enough room to make sure that they are covered from the light and protected. If the seed is exceptionally fine, then you can mix it with a little dry sand to help get even distribution when you sprinkle it over the surface of the trough. You then cover it with more sand in the usual way.

Space seeds a little closer together than the instructions on the packet tell you to do. You can always pack more into a hydroponic garden than in an ordinary one. In the case of larger things like beans or peas, it's a good idea to plant a third more than you have room for, as some may not germinate. And when the shoots come up

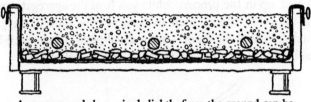

A greengrocer's box raised slightly from the ground can be
used for soil-less culture

you can easily eliminate the weaker ones (with no weeds coming up alongside them, it's much easier to spot the plants). On the flower front, plant seeds close together to get a good display; remember you're less likely to get weaklings since they are being specially fed with nutrient. Carnations and chrysanthemums are positive naturals for being grown this way – most of the flowers you see on sale in florists' shops have been grown hydroponically. Bulbs will take perfectly happily to hydroponics too; indeed hyacinths that are grown in special glass containers are basically being raised in that way.

Once you've planted your container, the next job is to water the surface lightly, using some form of spray or sprinkler so that you won't disturb the freshly sown seed. If you haven't a watering can at the moment (you'll certainly need one eventually) you could use a shower attachment with the water (cold, of course) only just turned on. Since the growing medium has already been well soaked and drained beforehand, this last watering should be just enough to moisten the surface.

Transplanting seedlings into a soil-less trough

It's perfectly possible to transplant seedlings that you've grown elsewhere, or bought from a garden centre into a hydroponic unit. But first you must wash away any trace of soil from the roots to avoid possible contamination or souring of the aggregate. The easiest way to do this is to hold the plant gently by its stem, between your thumb and forefinger, under a running tap. Then you simply make a hole in the aggregate with a pencil or a piece of stick, wiggling it a little as you push it in, to make space for root-spread. Now push the seedling in, with one hand, taking care that its roots don't get folded back up in the process, while you firm the aggregate around it with the other. Roots need to be aerated – indeed, oxygen is absolutely essential for them – but a small plant, like a small baby, likes to be firmly wrapped up in something to feel secure.

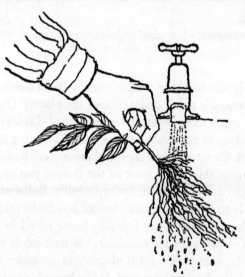

Wash away the soil from a seedling before
planting in a hydroponic unit

How to feed your plants

Twenty-four hours after you have sown the seed or put in the seedling, it's time to give the plant its first feed. The essential fertilising salts that are needed are sodium nitrate, potassium sulphate, superphosphate, magnesium sulphate and a trace of iron sulphate. It's perfectly feasible to buy these ingredients from a chemist or a garden supplier, or to get them mixed up specially for you in their correct proportions but a quicker and easier way of getting your plant food on tap is to buy a proprietary brand like Phostrogen, for instance, that is readily available, comes in several different-sized packets and is so concentrated that a teaspoonful will be enough for 2 gallons of water.

You can also get several different forms of mixture in tablet form; a tablet implanted in the medium near the roots of the plant will keep it happy for some time and all you need to do is water in the usual way. Otherwise, it pays to have a watering can of the mixture made up and ready on hand for topping up your troughs when you think they need watering. In hot weather or in a centrally heated house this can be daily, but usually two or three times a week is enough. The aim is to keep the surface of the medium just damp – rather like a damp wrung-out flannel – but never waterlogged.

Once a week, or any time when you suspect you may have over-watered your plants, remove the plugs or seals and allow the container to drain for about an hour. It may be that no moisture will seep through, but this operation has a fringe benefit – it allows air to penetrate the aggregate and get at the roots to ensure healthy growth. Once in a while – about every fortnight or three weeks, it's a good idea to flush the aggregate through to get rid of any unused plant food that may have accumulated and could go sour. To do this you simply take out the plugs, and give it a good dose of plain water.

Things to grow without soil

What can you grow hydroponically? Almost anything. The conventional house plants respond particularly well to this kind of culture but so too do bedding plants, bulbs and geraniums; vermiculite or sand, or a mixture of both, are especially good for rooting geranium cuttings. You can grow roses this way and old-fashioned cottagey flowers like stocks, sweet peas and marigolds. You can even grow azaleas, citrus plants and exotics like bougainvillea using this method, while the common or garden nasturtium comes in useful not just as a flower but for use in salads as well.

Jardinierès and special flower troughs lend themselves particularly well to soil-less culture, and if you put a small plastic bowl into a hanging basket, disguising it from the outside with a lining of sphagnum moss, you can use that for hydroponics as well. (I've had great success with those containers made from soft plastic that you buy for use in 'fridges and freezers, using Plasticine for plugs to keep in the moisture.) Using a hanging basket this way gets over the old bugbear – that it dries out so quickly you're apt to overlook it for a day or so and then find that the plants have died. Window boxes, too, benefit from being used for hydroponic culture, since if you use vermiculite in the medium their weight is reduced and they're less likely to do damage to a rickety wooden window sill.

An easy, very basic form of hydroponics that many of us tried as children is planting the cut-off top of any root vegetable – carrot, beetroot or parsnip for instance, in a saucer with a few pebbles to support it and water half-way up the side. For the frustrated flat-dweller with nothing more than one tiny window sill this is the quickest way of getting instant greenery in winter. Carrots make a marvellous impromptu table decoration since they produce foliage that looks like maidenhair fern in a matter of days. On a more sophisticated level, if you buy a fresh pineapple with its top in a reasonable condition, you can slice that off, just like a carrot top, and start it off in a saucer of damp aggregate. Who knows, you might end up with a respectable-sized plant; it can be done if you keep it in a warm, light place.

Herbs and salads

It's perhaps in the kitchen that hydroponics comes into its own as a really practical way to grow things. Too often herbs get relegated to the end of the garden and are therefore seldom used. Even in a mini town garden it can be too much trouble on a dark rainy night to go out and cut some rosemary for the lamb or a *bouquet garni* to liven up a salad or stew. But have them growing on your own window sill and you're inspired to new culinary heights. Fortunately, herbs are among the easiest things to grow without soil. Even fiery horseradish can be confined to a pot, while garlic, mint, tarragon and thyme will do well too. If you've the space, a large trough or a small stone sink planted with herbs looks particularly good either just outside or in the kitchen – if you can bring them indoors, and they have enough light to get by, you can sow the more exotic herbs like coriander in succession all year round.

Salads are a good starter in hydroponics, especially if you haven't much experience in vegetable gardening. It's a rewarding occupation because the different ingredients grow so well together. Lettuces respond particularly well to growing in a soil-less medium, and love the frequent doses of nutrient they are given. The essence of a good lettuce is that it should grow quickly so that the leaves are succulent and tender and not tough, and the extra rapid growth they get this way makes them an ideal candidate for the kitchen window sill. Plant slower-growing things like radishes first, use the lettuce as a 'catch-crop' planted in between, say, radishes and spring onions and you've a ready-made salad to hand.

From asparagus to strawberries

Asparagus sounds wildly improbable as the kind of thing one can grow on a balcony or in a flat, but it is possible with the help of hydroponics. To save time, buy a crown or two rather than a packet of seeds – asparagus doesn't start producing anything until its third year. This is where useful fast-growing things like the lettuce come in, for you can plant shallow-rooting crops between the crowns without any harm. Asparagus positively laps up the nutrient you give it and will, in fact, do better grown in a soil-less medium with maximum attention to feeding than in indifferent surroundings in an ordinary garden. When the time comes to blanch the first crop of shoots, put a wrapping of plastic round the stems to exclude the light and make sure that they remain white.

You're not likely to want to grow potatoes in a flat or a really small garden, but if you enjoy flying in the face of Nature, and like the taste of really young potatoes – even if you only have them for one or two meals – you can grow them very successfully by using hydroponics and at the same time cut out all the problem of searching for the new potatoes in the ground. Just make a hole in the aggregate as you would for planting a bulb, make sure the seed potatoes are well covered with it, sit back and wait!

Another item well worth trying is the alpine strawberry which can be forced by being grown indoors on aggregate. Be careful though that the leaves don't get too waterlogged when you are feeding with nutrient solution – always a problem in the case of any plant that clings close to the ground. The highly flavoured tiny strawberries can be brought on, early in the season, if you put each cluster into a jam-jar which acts as a miniature cloche around them.

The tomato, which could be described as a gross feeder, responds well to soil-less culture. In fact, a lot of amateur growers are already raising their plants hydroponically without realising it. Remember, the more warmth and light you can give them, the better and earlier crop you'll get – after all, who wants home-grown tomatoes when there's a glut in the shops? A brick wall makes an ideal back-drop for tomato raising, and if you germinate the seedlings early in shallow trays of the vermiculite-sand mix, indoors, you're well on the way to beating the greengrocer at his own game.

House plants without soil

Supposing you are given a house plant for Christmas and you want to keep it going hydroponically, is it possible to make the switch? Yes, if you disinfect the plant first. It sounds like being over-fussy, but the essence of soil-less culture is that all risk of disease and bacteria is eliminated. How do you disinfect your new aquisition? Quite simply, with the help of Jeyes' Fluid. Just douse the plant once or twice in a solution of 1 fluid ounce of the disinfectant to 2½ pints of water, then plant it carefully in its new home. This hint comes from James Sholto Douglas's useful book *The Beginner's Guide to Hydroponics* (Pelham Books, £2.25) – required reading for anyone who wants to take up this type of gardening seriously. He also gives you an idea of the vast range of possibilities by describing how you can grow anything from orchids to mushrooms this way. So you can't be too ambitious!

10 Ways of Stretching Space

I S IT *really* possible to stretch space in a tiny back yard or a roof garden, or a balcony for that matter, by the use of illusion? Emphatically, yes. One of the rather more expensive but undoubtedly effective tricks you can play is with the aid of mirrors, as I'll explain later, but you can do a lot with cunning landscaping and planting too, as I've already suggested in Chapter 8.

We're used to seeing a pine tree at a certain height, for instance, so that whenever we look at one, our eyes tend to assume that it must be tall. Plant a small-scale conifer at the end of a small garden, therefore and because of its size we immediately imagine it is further away than it actually is – by the same token making the garden appear larger too. Add dwarf versions of familiar flowers like the Michaelmas daisy and the daffodil (the 'hoop petticoat' is a good one to choose) and the illusion is complete; try it in one corner of your patio if you don't believe me.

A pool makes a garden seem larger, too, because of the other dimension, depth, that it brings. Another quick trick in planting is to take your cue from the artist's way of making things farthest from the eye darker and deeper in colour than those near to you. Edge your garden or yard with dark evergreens, especially the small conifers in blue-green shades, then plant paler-coloured shrubs in front. The area will immediately appear to have more depth than before and give the illusion of being larger.

Creating false perspective
Using curves generously is another good way of enlarging the tiniest garden, especially if it is inclined to be narrow too. The longer the eye takes to travel along a line, the farther away it will seem to be, so you can enlarge the apparent area of a place by cleverly placed flower beds or troughs jutting out from the side so that they hide

the path in places and break a long narrow yard into a series of areas or separate rooms. A path that meanders or sweeps round to its destination will make anything look wider and longer than it really is, particularly if you hide the actual end of it in a bed of shrubs, giving the illusion that it carries on beyond the wall.

If you are stuck with a straight path for practical reasons, however, all is not lost; if you narrow it progressively towards the far end it will create a false perspective, for we are so used to straight paths narrowing at a certain rate that if that is accelerated we imagine them to be longer than they really are. This trick only works seen from the broad end, so start it that way at the house.

Given a solid wall there's a lot you can do to open it out and give a hint of more garden behind. Try, for instance, painting it white with a series of big sweeping arches, almost like a viaduct, then filling in the gaps between the arches with a darker colour – a mixture of brown and black is good. It should be a matt paint, incidentally, such as an outdoor emulsion, nothing shiny. The dark colour looks realistically like the gloom inside a covered walk or a terrace and you can soften up the stark lines with a climber or two – plant one or two bushes in front, so what goes on at ground level is not too apparent and it really will seem that the wall is a series of arches with a covered passageway behind.

Deceiving the eye
Getting more complicated, *trompe l'oeil* arches can be made from pieces of plastic drainpipe painted white, set in wooden plinths at

A solid wall can be painted to look like a series of arches

intervals along the wall and topped by a series of wooden arches and a wooden top. Once you've made a template to cut round for the first arch, the rest are easy to get alike. Another idea is to use wrought iron screen work (a firm in the Isle of Wight is now reproducing panels of lacy Victorian patterns) placed just an inch or so in front of a wall that has been painted a dark colour to give a three-dimensional effect.

Paint a giant smiling sun face on a narrow back yard wall

You can of course hire a professional artist to paint a real *trompe l'oeil* gateway or arch on your wall but this has to be very well done to succeed and therefore might well cost you a great deal of money. A simple garden decoration I've seen which you could easily have a go at yourself is a giant fake Rousseau-esque jungle of plants and ferns painted in deep green against a white wall at the end of a terrace, with real plants such as *Yucca gloriosa* and *Fatsia japonica*, or a fig, just in front. This works amazingly well, no matter how amateurishly the leaves are painted. Try it for yourself in a powder poster colour that will wash off if necessary and move some pot plants in front – I think you'll find you are pleased with the result. Another idea I've seen is Pop Art in origin and makes a cheerful ending for a plain back yard. It's a giant smiling sun painted in yellow with multicoloured rays coming from it at the end of a rather narrow, miserable yard – the effect is electrifying. If you daren't attempt to paint it on the wall yourself, no doubt your local art school could suggest a student who would do the job for a reasonable fee.

By night it is easy to stretch a garden with lighting – put floods so that they point up the trees and shrubs, leave the outer perimeter of a patio in darkness and it looks almost endless. In the same way if your terrace is rather bald and unfurnished as yet, well-directed lights in a small space will make it seem more intimate, while flood-lights on a balcony make a marvellous view if you are dining by the window.

Extending your view

By day, reviving the old idea of a ha-ha works in some cases when *your* garden or yard is tiny but there is plenty of space beyond. A ha-ha is quite simply a fence or hedge set in a deep ditch either side, at the end of a garden, which makes it impossible for animals and people to get through but doesn't interrupt the view, giving the householder the illusion that his yard or garden stretches right to the horizon. If your garden overlooks a park or open countryside that's fine, but if there is someone else's garden backing on to yours, a certain amount of goodwill and digging is required for this plan to work. I know a man who made doubly sure that his ha-ha was burglar proof – he dug a deep ditch, set his fence of chain-link and rambler roses in a concrete trough, and filled his side of the ditch with water to deter all comers.

Even a piece of statuary, provided it is of a good quality (*not*, please not, a gnome) placed on an end wall in an arch of a dark colour edged with ivy will give the illusion that the garden goes on further than it does, especially if you floodlight it at night; in a small garden this need not cost much. For what we are trying to do is to

A ha-ha creates a barrier without interrupting the view

lead the eye on farther, beyond the actual boundaries of the patio or yard. The same trick perspective I mentioned earlier, narrowing a path towards the far end, can be done equally well with a pergola too. Place your arches or frames closer together as they get further away from the house or flat, make each one minimally lower than the next – the first should be above normal height in this case to allow for this – and when their bare bones are covered with roses and clematis or a vine, they will appear to stretch far away into the distance.

Add a touch of fantasy

A tiny gazebo or summerhouse is an attractive, space-stretching addition to a small yard; make it semi-circular in shape with the straight side against a wall and it will appear to enlarge the garden. Apart from purely practical uses like the storing of a moped, garden tools and odds and ends, it could become a pleasant place to sit in if it gets the sun. A friend of mine who lives in Morocco had one built in his tiny garden in the shape of a marabout, a Moslem shrine, with arched walls and a fretwork decoration. Using local labour it cost him little or nothing – anyone who is handy with brickwork and a fretsaw could do the same – and he keeps his bicycle and his garden tools in it.

After all, when you come to think of it, a toolshed doesn't *have* to look like a toolshed; it could be shaped like a pagoda for instance.

A short cut to a livelier look is to buy the framework of a hexagonal greenhouse, paint it white, add some decoration, and take it from there. It's simply a question of spending a little more money but mainly more time and trouble. The same could go for a garage, too, if it impinges on the back yard. The design facing the street could be perfectly conventional but there's nothing to stop you having a fantasy roof and walls at the back, or elongating it to make a covered barbecue area, as long as you put asbestos on the communicating wall with the car.

Make your wall interesting
There are lots of other ideas around for decorating dull walls. You could, for instance, fix a full-blown mediaeval-looking door on it, or a Georgian-style one complete with fanlight or pediment overhead. These can now be bought quite easily off the peg complete even with columns and plinths. Fix it firmly though, for people are sure to try and open it! Even a large wrought iron gate bought second hand from a scrap merchants could be placed against a dark piece of wall to open it up.

Another simple idea to add interest to a high brick wall, the kind you so often get in a town garden, is to add 'battlements' on top, in fact nothing more than breeze blocks cemented on at regular intervals (you'll have to get your next-door neighbour's permission, of course). Encourage ivy to swarm over it for long-term effect – it will make the wall look very old, almost mediaeval, but meanwhile use a swift growing creeper (see Chapter 2) for instant effect.

Another way to make a wall look livelier is to put a series of troughs on the top planted with flowering climbers which will cascade down for a 'hanging-garden-of-Babylon' look, with perhaps others coming up to meet them from below. Remember, though, if the wall is at all exposed to the elements, especially wind, the creepers will need fixing in place if they are not going to toss like a curtain in a gale and possibly break off.

It's all done by mirrors
You can do an enormous amount with mirrors if you have walls of solid brick or concrete – they don't really work on fences. But it's a

(Top) Fix a Georgian-style door to a blank wall. (Centre) Creeper-covered battlements, made of breeze blocks, lend a mediaeval look. (Bottom) Fake a 'window' in a boring wall by fixing a mirror, then framing it and adding a wrought iron grille

good idea first to see if your local glass merchant and mirror man can offer a special backing for them that is weatherproof. If he can't help you can, at a pinch, simply stick strips of Fablon or something similar on the back – even vinyl wallpaper – to stop them flaking. This sort of material certainly helps preserve them.

It is perhaps on a balcony that a mirror especially comes into its own, more than anywhere else, especially if it is protected from the weather. If you have solid, full-height walls on either side, as so many modern blocks of flats have, then if you cover each one with a mirror so that they reflect each other, put some interesting plants in front and train creepers round to hide the edges, your balcony will appear to more than double in size; the reflections are endless. If you don't believe me, borrow a couple of mirrors and try it for yourself before having any custom-made.

A mirror can hint at all sorts of delights beyond; it can masquerade as a window or as an archway, or simply as a hole in the wall. The main thing to do to make it believable is to disguise its rather obvious edge, either with a false front or architraves round it, a course of bricks, perhaps in an arch, or simply a climbing plant. One way or another, you must hide those sharp edges.

One of the cheapest ways to use a mirror is to pick a fairly small one, fix it on a wall and cover it with a real window frame or a wrought iron Spanish-style grille, turning it into a window in the wall. Site and angle your mirror carefully so that it doesn't distort what you see or reflect you directly (which gives the game away immediately) or focus on a view that you wouldn't want to see anyway, like dustbins or a back door. Place some tall plants in front – you'll see them twice, once as they actually are, once in a reflection – and it's amazing how different they look that way. A large mirror with a wrought iron gate in front of it, even if it only comes half-way up, can be made to look like a doorway or archway or, if a simple brick arch is built round it, like a way through into another section of the garden.

Tricks with trellis
Treillage, using trellis to disguise a wall and give illusions or to cordon off a part of a garden, has been used since Elizabethan times

and is a positive gift to the owner of a tiny town garden. Ordinary diamond-shaped trellis by the yard is fine if you merely want to jazz up a wall or provide cover for climbers, but for anything more ambitious you really need the squared off variety, plus trellis battens, which can be bought in most big do-it-yourself timber merchants.

One of the easiest ways of giving an illusion with trellis battening is to make it appear that the wall goes in towards a gateway or a statue. And here you must work out your perspective carefully if it is to succeed. Decide on a 'vanishing point' in the middle of a fake arch or doorway, at eye level, mark it with a piece of chalk, then radiate four trellis battens around an arch shape, so that if the line was continued they would in fact touch the chalk mark. It's just like drawing something in perspective, using the usual rules.

Having worked out that basic principle, fixing the battens is merely a matter of trial and error. You need two people for this job, one to hold the batten up in place, the other (with a keen eye) to see if it looks all right, then nail it. Fix the top centre battens first (it is best in fact to have one on either side of the centre point) and then two half-way up the sides, then fill in the rest and you will find it relatively easy. Remember the more sharply the battens slope inwards, the deeper the archway is going to appear. To finish the effect you must add a curved batten to cover the outer ends, better still one to cover the inner ends too.

Even more ambitious is the *trompe l'oeil* wall made from battens that curve inwards, but this requires some skill since you have to steam them first to get them to go the way you want them. A whole wall of trellis, a mixture of radiating battens, squared off panels and a mirror in the centre with a statue in front can create the perfect illusion that the end wall of a garden is merely a gateway through to more exciting things beyond. Try it for yourself and see.

11 Making Much of Your Stock

PROVIDED YOU'VE done the right thing and given them the best soil you can get, your plants should flourish in small containers or beds in a town atmosphere. But there are one or two things to watch. Watering comes first. Any plant that is raised in unnatural conditions – e.g., in a trough, a raised bed on concrete, a window box or a basket can rarely rely on a natural water supply to keep it going. In summer a basket or a window box will usually need doing daily – sometimes twice a day in a heatwave. You can save yourself some trouble by moving your containers away from the shelter of a roof or some other cover if rain is threatened, in the hope that they will get a good soaking. Always use a watering can on small plants; the only exceptions are those that are well-established or things like the geranium or the auricula, which hates getting its flowers too wet. Using a jug or a hose over small seedlings will simply swamp and drown them, knocking them over with the force of the water. Buy the best watering-can you can get – plastic ones have an irritating habit of getting their roses silted up and there is no real substitute for a metal one.

If you're living in town conditions then evergreens will need their leaves sponging or cleaning from time to time – when they begin to look dry and dusty either flick them over with a feather duster, or shake them and give them a fine spray of water. The third thing to remember is that even though you may be in the centre of a city you're not going to be free from pests; an oasis of luscious food such as you are providing for greenfly, blackfly and the rest is not going to be passed over lightly. I don't know quite where they come from but they will certainly seek you out. So you'll find that in time you'll have to acquire quite a battery of pesticides to cope with them. Fortunately, concentrated as the plants are in a small space, it doesn't take long to spray them but a small spray pack which you pump up and which gives a fine mist makes the whole job a great deal easier, if you are moving from one site to another with it.

Growing from seed

Growing your own plants from seed is fun, if you have the space, but in a flat or any confined area what to do with seed trays and boxes becomes something of a problem. The same goes for taking cuttings too. But if you plant them in pots and give them the miniature greenhouse treatment (see page 42) you can leave most of them outside, or at least accelerate their growth on a window sill. The idea is quite simple. Having planted your seeds and watered them, you cover them with a balloon of plastic so that they have a micro-climate of their own inside. They are kept moist because water that evaporates will condense on the side of the plastic and run back into the soil again; the plastic balloon is a particularly useful trick with all plants if you go away at weekends. The extra heat they get from the polythene covering – more so if it is somewhere light and sunny – will bring the plants on quickly too.

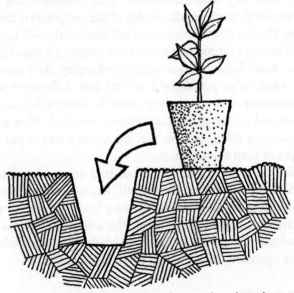

Save pricking out seedlings by growing them in paper pots which can later be planted out directly

It's worthwhile spending money on sterilised soil such as John Innes Compost No 1 for seedlings. For one thing you know then that anything green that comes up must be your seed that you planted – using ordinary garden soil means that you're probably nurturing weeds, stinging nettles even, in their infancy to the detriment of the real plant you want to grow and it's difficult to tell which is which until they get their second set of leaves. What you *can* save money on is containers. Seeds will grow happily in anything – an empty tin, the cartons that held yoghurt or cream or peanut butter or honey. Or better still you can use those compressed paper pots you can buy from garden centres. Planted in paper pots the precious seeds can be transferred just as they are into a garden bed, a tub or a window box without the rather agonising process of 'pricking out' when you gingerly lift up the seedling and place it in its new home.

If you are sowing largish seeds like morning glory, beans, peas, nasturtiums, soak them overnight in slightly warm water to soften up their seed coats and then sow double the quantity you eventually require, since they tend sometimes not to germinate. It's then a simple matter to pinch out the weaker of the two plants if they both come up. Having planted your seeds and watered the soil, now place a plastic bag over the top of the container, securing it round the side with an elastic band or some tightly tied string. As I mentioned before, when using polythene it is vital that it does not actually come into direct contact with the plant or the leaves will immediately frizzle up and go brown for they become scorched. Blow into the bag if necessary to inflate it, so that it acts like a tent or put a twig in the pot to keep it up high.

If you have to prick your plants out later on, use a pointed nail file or a plastic plant label for the job. Remember they may have made quite long roots, so prod well down below the surface and lift them carefully, digging up some of the soil as well as the roots. Make holes in the new containers in which they are to go before you start this operation, then you can drop plants straight in.

Storing cuttings

Taking cuttings need not take up too much space and gives plants a much swifter start in life. There's no need even to plant them in soil at first. Get a strip of black plastic, put a strip of damp moss along it, lengthwise, dip your cuttings in special hormone rooting powder and place them at intervals on your plastic strip so that their leaves are well clear of the top edge and the ends which are to root right in the centre of the damp moss. Turn up the lower edge of the plastic to encase the roots safely, roll up your strip like a tool kit, secure it with string and your cuttings are stowed away nicely and will start growing almost immediately. Don't leave them in direct sunlight or the heat may burn the delicate area where the cuts have been made; they need light, however, to thrive.

Citrons like orange, lemon or tangerine can be grown very success-fully from seed, if you have the patience; they take a long time to get started. Soak the seed in warm water overnight, put it in a container, give it the polythene treatment and wait. It may take several weeks for them to come up but eventually they will oblige. The avocado pear stone makes a marvellous lush green plant not unlike the rubber plant but that, too, takes some getting going. The best way to start it is in one of those special glass containers made for growing hyacinths in water. Put it in with the pointed end downwards and make sure that the tip only *just* brushes the surface of the water, cover the jar with a polythene bag and wait. A pineapple can be propagated to make a handsome plant – you could even get fruit from it if you keep it indoors behind glass, somewhere sunny. Instructions for growing it hydroponically are in Chapter 9; use some hormone rooting powder on it to get it going.

Increasing your stock

If you want to increase your stock of shrubs or you've been able to persuade a friend to give you a cutting to grow, remember that you must take the wood from this year's growth. The shoots should be soft or semi-ripe and you should go for a short-jointed stocky one rather than something long and spindly. Choose the part of the bush that has had the most sunlight, too, rather than a side in the shade. The best mixture for rooting small shrubby cuttings in is a 50–50 com-bination of peat and sand. The plant can stay in this for two months or so until it is properly established. It should root within a fortnight.

Choose your container and put some ash or gravel in the bottom for drainage, then half fill it with a mixture of peat and sand. Water the growing medium and leave it for an hour to settle. Take your cutting by making as clean a cut as you can – it is usually done on the slant, with a razor or a very sharp penknife, making it just below a joint on the stem of the plant. Remove the bottom two leaves, damp the end and slip it in hormone rooting powder, then shake off any surplus and put it in a hole prepared beforehand by a small dibber or a stick. See that it sits comfortably in its hole, then gently firm the soil round it with your fingers. Now water it with a fine rose on the watering can and cover the container with a polythene bag. If you are putting several cuttings into a box, then a sheet of glass placed over the top will do just as well. Leave your cuttings in semi-shade to get going. If this is impossible then cover them with newspaper until the first fortnight is over and they have taken root. At 8–12 weeks later they will be ready for re-potting or putting out in place.

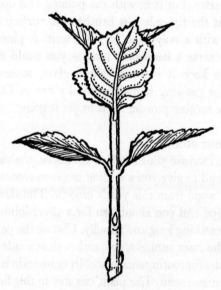

Taking a cutting

Layering a shrub

Layering is an easy way to increase some climbers and plants like the rhododendron and the azalea. Take a good-looking well-grown shoot (this year's growth again), nick it about a third of the way through, underneath, dip it in hormone powder and then carefully bury this section of the branch (but not the end as well) in the ground beside the plant; alternatively, more convenient, bury it in a pot – a useful dodge if the branch you have chosen won't bend easily to the ground. Weigh the buried section down with a stone or something heavy. Although it is still attached to the mother plant, the cut section of the stem will eventually form its own roots. Once it is well under way – wait a month or so – you can turn it into a separate plant.

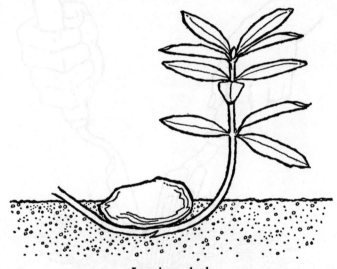

Layering a shrub

Lots of other herbaceous plants, the Michaelmas daisy for instance, and anything bushy like that can be increased simply by division – indeed they need to be divided or they will choke themselves to death. This is a perfectly simple operation. All you do is to shove a hand fork and a trowel or two large kitchen forks deep into the central mass of the plant, back to back, then pull them apart

One half can then be shifted somewhere else or given away to a gardening friend.

One last thought on the subject of propagation, although it is not strictly that: you can divide up clumps of herbs in the autumn, replant half of them hydroponically in containers and force them in the winter, so you have an all year round supply. Just bring them into a warm room and keep their soil slightly moist and after a week or so they will start to grow again and make new leaves.

The right tools for the job
It definitely pays to have the proper tools for small space gardening, since you will need so few. You *can* use things from the kitchen and

Increasing a plant by division

indeed, I have a whole host of bent fish fryers, forks and serving spoons that I have pressed into service for window box work in an emergency. But the truth is that you *do* damage them, and even if you invest in a splendid stainless steel trowel and fork it is not going to set you back all that much. A coarse sieve is a useful thing to have too, if you are just beginning on your gardening career, because it enables you to sift the earth that you get from other gardens, or from friends, to get rid of the lumps. Another invaluable item is a set of plant labels and a waterproof marker (though I find an ordinary pencil or Biro is really almost as good). In the first flush of spring enthusiasm it is easy to rush round sowing seeds here and there – and then forget what you've put in where so you don't know how to treat it when it comes up.

12 Plants for Small Space Gardening

HERE IS a detailed list of plants which are specially suitable for small space gardening, some of which have been mentioned in previous chapters together with many other suggestions. They are grouped so that you can easily discover which plants you have a good chance of growing in particular sites such as window boxes, patios or pools, and in problem corners which may be dark and shady or sun-baked and dry. Those which require special soil conditions are given separately. Most of the plants listed are obtainable at any good garden centre.

HT=height	Sun and shade requirements
D/E=deciduous/evergreen	
D=deciduous	○=full sun
E=evergreen	◑=partial shade
(S)=semi-evergreen	●=shade

PERMANENT PLANTS

Botanical Name	Common Name	Habit	Sun/Shade	Soil
BUXUS *sempervirens*	common box	compact rounded clump	◐ to ●	any
sempervirens 'Aurea'	golden box	compact rounded clump	◐ to ●	any
HEBE *armstrongii*	shrubby Veronica	upright spreading	○ to ◐	any
'Autumn Glory'		spreading	○ to ◐	any
'Midsummer Beauty'		spreading	○ to ◐	any
pinguifolia 'Pagei'		compact	○ to ◐	any
HEDERA *helix* varieties	common ivy	matty climber	◐ to ●	any
See also Plants for Shade				
Roses, miniature		upright spreading	○ to ◐	rich, good drain essential
VINCA *minor*	lesser periwinkle	carpet rooting	◐ to ●	any

SEASONAL PLANTS

Botanical Name	Common Name	Habit	Sun/Shade	Soil
ANTIRRHINUM dwarf bedding varieties	snapdragon	bushy	○ to ◐	any not too alkalin
BEGONIA *semperflorens* compact varieties		compact	○ to ◐	fibrous
CALLISTEPHUS *chinensis* dwarf varieties	China aster	bush	○	ordinary
CALCEOLARIA most varieties	slipper flower	bushy	○ to ◐	ordinary
CELOSIA dwarf varieties	coxscomb	bushy	○ to ◐	ordinary
CENTAUREA *cyanus* all varieties	cornflower	upright	○	ordinary
imperialis		upright	○	ordinary

ht/Spread	D/E	Foliage	Flower	Fruit	Comments
2 ft	E	dark green, golden or variegated			
p 2 ft	E	golden yellow margins			
p 1 ft	E	olive green	very small white July/Aug		
2 ft	E	purplish green	blue June/Oct		many other good varieties but these are easier to grow
2 ft	E	light green	lavender June/Sep		
3 ft	E	glaucous green	white May/June		
⁀ 1–5 ft	E	bright green, golden, variegated			most varieties suitable
9 in	D		white, pinks, reds, mauves, yellows June/Sep		most varieties suitable. Could not interplant with seasonal plants
1½ ft	E	glossy green	blue June/Aug		
9 in			mixed June/Oct		plant May/June
6–8 in		bright green to deep bronze	white to deep scarlet June/Oct		plant May/June
n 8–12 in			blues, pinks, whites		plant May/June
in 8–12 in		usually soft green	reds and yellows June/Aug		plant May/June
t 1 ft		rich greens	yellow to red feathery plumes June/Sep		plant June
t		spiky, often silvery	pale blue to deep scarlet June/Sep		sow seed direct, March on
			all colours June/Sep		sow seed direct, March on

SEASONAL PLANTS—*cont.*

Botanical Name	Common Name	Habit	Sun/Shade	Soil
CHEIRANTHUS *allionii* dwarf bedding varieties	Siberian wallflower	bushy	○ to ◑	ordinary
CHRYSANTHEMUM *frutescens*	marguerites, Paris daisy	bushy	○	ordinary
COLEUS dwarf varieties		bush	○ to ◑	ordinary
FUCHSIA varieties		bushy shrubs	○ to ◑	ordinary
GAZANIA varieties	treasure flower	spreading	○	light sandy
HELIOTROPIUM varieties	heliotrope	bushy	◑	rich sandy
IPOMOEA varieties	morning glory	trailing climber	○	rich
LATHYRUS *odoratus* varieties	sweet pea	twining climber	○ to ◑	rich sandy
LOBELIA trailing varieties		trailing, spreading	○ to ◑	ordinary
MATTHIOLA annual varieties	ten-week stock	bushy	○	light
bicornis	night-scented stock	open bush	○	light
incana varieties	Brompton or winter stock	bushy	○	light
MESEMBRYANTHEMUM *criniflorum*	Livingstone daisy	spreading	○	light sandy
NEMESIA varieties		bushy	○	ordinary
NICOTIANA dwarf varieties	tobacco plant	upright	○ to ●	ordinary

ght/Spread		D/E	Foliage	Flower	Fruit	Comments
5 in	9 in	E		yellows, oranges and reds March/May		plant Oct
	2½ ft	E		white and yellow June/Sep		plant May; tender can be over-wintered, also grown as standard
ft	1–2 ft	E	all colours	purplish, insignificant		plant June; very tender; can be overwintered
ft	1½–3 ft	D	bright green to purples	white, pinks to deep purples June/Oct		plant June; can be trained as standards
5 in	1–1½ ft	E		yellow, pink, scarlet July/Oct		plant June
ft	1–1½ ft	E	dull green	pale blue, lavender June/Sep		can be trained as standards
5 ft				blues, whites June/Sep		plant May/June very prolific climber
ft				most colours June/Sep		plant June; need support
5 in			bright green and purplish tints	white, blues, reds June/Oct		plant May/June
	1 ft			white, lavenders, purples, reds. scented June/July		plant May
	9 in		greyish green	lavender, scented June/July		plant May
	1–1½ ft			white, blues, pinks March/May		plant March
	15 in		glaucous, fleshy	pinks to rich orange July/Sep		plant June
in	6–12 in			blues, pinks, yellows, orange, scarlets June/Sep		plant May/June
	1 ft		large, dull green	white, crimsons, lime greens July/Sep		plant May/June

Botanical Name	Common Name	Habit	Sun/Shade	Soil
PELARGONIUM zonal most varieties	geranium	bush	○ to ◑	rich loam
ivy leaf varieties		trailing	○ to ◑	rich loam
PETUNIA varieties		spreading	○ to ◑	ordinary
SALVIA varieties		upright	○ to ◑	ordinary
TAGETES	African marigolds	upright	○	ordinary
	French marigolds	cushion	○	ordinary
VIOLA most varieties	pansies	cushion	○ to ◑	ordinary
ZINNIA all varieties	youth-and-old-age	upright or cushion	○	ordinary

CACTI

Most are tender but can be left outside from mid-June to September. Soil: well-drained sandy l
Some members of genus *Opuntia*, such as *O. compressa*, *O. engelmannii*, and *O. vulgaris* (Barbar
are completely hardy in well-drained sunny positions.

BULBS

Most bulbs such as anemones, chionodoxa, colchicum (meadow saffron), crocus, cyclamen, fre
galanthus (snowdrops), hyacinths, irises, narcissus (daffodils), scilla, and tulips are suitabl
window boxes. As a rule select dwarfer varieties as these are not so liable to wind damage. Soil sl
be rich, fibrous, and well-drained. Full sun to partial shade is desirable.

WATER PLANTS   FOR SMALL PON

Botanical Name	Common Name	Habit	Sun/Shade	Soil
AZOLLA *caroliniana*	fairy moss	moss-like carpet	○ to ◑	floating
CALLITRICHE *autumnalis*	water starwort	submerged spreading	○	heavy peaty-cla
HOTTONIA *palustris*	water violet	spiky erect	○	ordinary

ight/Spread		D/E	Foliage	Flower	Fruit	Comments
ft	1–2 ft	E	greens, purples, white, leaves zoned	white, pinks, reds, purples May/Oct		plant May/June
½ ft		E	ivy shaped, variegated usually	white, pinks, mauves June/Oct		ideal for hanging baskets plant May/June
½ ft	1 ft		soft green	white, pinks, reds, blues June/Sep		plant May/June
	1 ft		bright green	bright red spikes June/Sep		plant May/June
ft	1 ft		scented	pompon type blooms, lemon yellow to red May/Sep		plant May/June
2 in	6–12 in		scented	single and double, lemon yellow to red May/Sep		plant May/June
in	6–9 in	E		all colours March–Sep		plant Oct for spring or May/June for summer
ft	1–1½ ft			pompon type blooms, all colours June/Sep		plant May/June

D POOLS

ht/Spread	D/E	Foliage	Flower	Fruit	Comments
	(S)	soft green, turns red in autumn			increases rapidly by self-division
	(S)	pale green entirely submerged			plant in pans at base of pool; good oxygenator
	(S)	finely divided in whorls	soft lilac June/Aug		plant in shallow water

Botanical Name	Common Name	Habit	Sun/Shade	Soil
NYMPHAEA 'Aurora'	water lily	floating	○	ordinary
'Firecrest'		floating	○	ordinary
'Froebelii'		floating	○	ordinary
'Graziella'		floating	○	ordinary
'James Brydon'		floating	○ to ◑	ordinary
laydekeri 'Fulgens'		floating	○	ordinary
laydekeri 'Lilacea'		floating	○	ordinary
laydekeri 'Purpurata'		floating	○	ordinary
nitilda		floating	○	ordinary
odorata 'Sulphurea'		floating	○	ordinary
pygmaea alba		floating	○	ordinary
pygmaea 'Helvola'		floating	○	ordinary

MARGINAL AND PONDSIDE PLANTS

Botanical Name	Common Name	Habit	Sun/Shade	Soil
CALTHA *palustris*	marsh marigold or kingcup	clump	○ to ●	rich, wet
CYPRIPEDIUM *calceolus*	lady's slipper orchid	upright	○	cool rich moist
IRIS *cristata*		upright creeping	○	cool moist
forrestii		upright creeping	○	cool moist
kaempferi		upright creeping	○	cool moist to w
laevigata		upright spreading	○	wet
laevigata 'Snowdrift'		upright spreading	○	wet
pseudacorus	yellow water iris yellow water flag	upright spreading	○	wet
versicolor 'Kermesina'		upright spreading	○	wet
RANUNCULUS *lingua grandiflora*	spearwort	upright	○	wet
TROLLUS *europaeus*	globeflower	clump	○ to ◑	cool rich moist

t/Spread	D/E	Foliage	Flower	Fruit	Comments
	D	small, mottled purple	yellow turning orange		*water depths* 6–12 in
	D		deep pink very fragrant		1–1½ ft
	D		small blood red		1–1½ ft
	D	mottled purple	reddish-yellow		1–1½ ft
	D	purplish-green	carmine		1½–2 ft
ft	D		crimson		6 in–1½ ft
ft	D		rosy-lilac, fragrant		6 in–1½ ft
	D		rosy-crimson		1–1½ ft
t	D	bright green	white, scented		1½–2 ft
t	D	green blotched	deep yellow		1–1½ ft
t	D	bright green	small white		6 in–1 ft
t	D	green mottled texture	soft yellow		6 in–1 ft
1½ ft	D	rounded bright green	large golden March		
	D		chocolate brown and yellow May/June		
	D		bright lilac blotched orange May		
ft	D	grassy	soft yellow June/July		
½ ft	D		reddish purple and yellow June/July		
	D		blue purple June		
	D		pure white June/July		
	D		bright yellow May/June		
t	D		deep red May/June		
2 ft	D	bright green shaped spear	bright yellow June/Aug		
t	1½ ft	D	rich lush green	yellow May/June		

Botanical Name	Common Name	Habit	Sun/Shade	Soil
TYPHA *minima*	dwarf reedmace	erect	○	wet

FERNS—PONDSIDE

ONOCLEA *sensibilis*	American sensitive fern	spreader	◑	wet peaty
WOODWARDIA *areolata*	North American chain fern	clump	◑	rich swampy soil

Other species: see Plants for Acid Soils

FOR A TROPICAL LOO

TREES AND SHRUBS

Botanical Name	Common Name	Habit	Sun/Shade	Soil
ARUNDINARIA: see Plants for Shade				
CAMELLIA: see Plants for Acid Soils				
CHAENOMELES 'Knap Hill Scarlet'	flowering quince or japonica	spreading shrub	◑	any
'Nivalis'		spreading shrub	◑	any
'Rowallane Seedling'		spreading shrub	◑	any
CYTISUS *battandieri*	Moroccan broom	upright, has to be trained	○	sandy
EUCALYPTUS *gunnii*	gum tree	usually slender tree	○	well-drained fibrous
FATSHEDERA *lizei*		sprawling	◑ to ●	any
FATSIA *japonica*		erect spreading	◑ to ●	avoid lime
HIBISCUS *syriacus* all varieties	mallow or shrubby althaea	spreading	○	rich light
LIBOCEDRUS *chilensis*	Chilean cedar	small columnar tree	○	rich, well-drained
MAGNOLIA *denudata*	Yulan or lily tree	spreading shrub	○	rich light
PAEONIA *suffruticosa*	tree paeony	spreading	◑	rich heavy
TRACHYCARPUS *fortunei*	Chusan palm or windmill palm	spreading palm	○	rich sandy

ght/Spread	D/E	Foliage	Flower	Fruit	Comments
	D	narrow rush like	brown catkins Aug/Nov		very rampant
ft	D	rich green			spreads rapidly
ft 2 ft	D	rich brownish-green			

R PATIOS AND ROOFS

ght/Spread	D/E	Foliage	Flower	Fruit	Comments
5 ft	D		salmon-scarlet March/May	golden yellow Aug/Oct	planting against north or east wall advances flowering
6 ft	D		white March/May	golden yellow Aug/Oct	
6 ft	D		bright crimson March/May	golden yellow Aug/Oct	
12 ft 8 ft	D	silky	bright yellow scented June/July		excellent on any sunny wall
30 ft 8–12 ft	E	glaucous blue to greyish-green			protect from frost first two seasons
3 ft	E	dark green leathery	pale green Aug/Oct		
6 ft	E	large green	milky white Oct/Nov		
6 ft	D	dull green	variable Aug/Sep		
30 ft 8 ft	E	sea green			very slow growing
15 ft 15 ft	D	white, fragrant March/April			often makes a small tree
3 ft	D		white to purple April/May		some protection from spring frosts
8 ft	E	very large fan shaped	yellow	bluish-black marble shaped	

Botanical Name	Common Name	Habit	Sun/Shade	Soil
YUCCA *gloriosa*	Adam's needle	small spreading tree	○	well-drained

HERBACEOUS—HARDY BULBS

ACANTHUS *mollis latifolius*	bear's breech	spreading	○ to ●	ordinary
CORTADERIA *selloana*	pampas grass	tufted	○ to ◐	rich light
selloana pumila		tufted	○ to ◐	rich light
ERYNGIUM *tripartitum*	sea holly	spreading	○	sandy
variifolium		spreading	○	sandy
KNIPHOFIA *caulescens*	red-hot poker	tufted	○	rich
galpinii		tufted	○	rich
uvaria		tufted	○	rich
PAPAVER *orientalis* varieties	Oriental poppy	upright	○	light
nudicaule	Iceland poppy	upright	○	light
TIGRIDIA *pavonia* varieties	tiger iris, tiger lily	upright	○	rich sandy

EVERGREENS FOR A▶

TREES AND SHRUBS

Botanical Name	Common Name	Habit	Sun/Shade	Soil
ABELIA *floribunda*		rounded	○	chalky
grandiflora		rounded	○	chalky

AZALEA: see under Rhododendron in Plants for Acid Soils

AZARA *petiolaris*		upright spreading	◐	well-drained
BERBERIS *darwinii*		spreading thicket	◐ to ●	ordinary

ight/Spread		D/E	Foliage	Flower	Fruit	Comments
	6 ft	E	long narrow pointed	creamy white July/Sep		spasmodic flowerer
		D	spiky foliage	lavender blue June/Aug		good architectural merit
ft	3–4 ft	(S)	slender arching	silvery grey plumes Aug/Oct		
ft	3 ft	(S)	slender arching	silvery grey plumes Aug/Oct		
ft	3½ ft	E	jagged edged, bluish tinge	blue June/Aug		leaves form tight rosettes in winter
ft	2 ft	E	steely green with conspicuous white veins	whitish green June/Aug		
ft	3 ft	D	green grassy tufts	salmon rose June		
	1½ ft	D	green grassy tufts	orange Sep/Oct		
	3 ft	D	green grassy tufts	orange-red July/Aug		
3 ft		D	pale green	white, pinks and crimsons May/July		
		D	pale green	many colours May/Sep		
ft		D		white, yellows and reds July/Aug		plant bulbs March/April in sunny position

AR ROUND FOLIAGE

ight/Spread		D/E	Foliage	Flower	Fruit	Comments
	5 ft	(S)	glossy green	cherry red June		plant against warm wall
	4 ft	(S)	brilliant dark green	pink and white June/Sep		
o ft	6 ft	E	large leathery	yellow, fragrant Feb/March		
	4–5 ft	E	small glossy holly-like	orange yellow April/May	bluish berries Aug/Nov	

Botanical Name	Common Name	Habit	Sun/Shade	Soil
BERBERIS *pruinosa*		spreading	◐ to ●	ordinary
CAMELLIA: see Plants for Acid Soils				
CARPENTERIA *californica*	Californian mock orange	upright spreading	○	light
CEANOTHUS 'Autumnal Blue'		upright	○	light
veitchianus		upright	○	light
CHOISYA *ternata*	Mexican orange blossom	rounded	◐	light peaty
CISTUS most varieties and species	rock rose	hummock	○	well-drained
CLIANTHUS *puniceus*	parrot's bill or lobster claw plant	upright spreading	○	rich fibrous
CONIFERS most genera		spreading	○	rich sandy
CONVOLVULUS *cneorum*		hummock	○	well-drained
COTONEASTER *lactes*		upright spreading	◐	ordinary
microphyllus		prostrate	◐	ordinary
salicifolius 'Autumn Fire'		prostrate	◐ to ●	ordinary
DESFONTAINEA *spinosa*		upright spreading	◐	peaty
DAPHNE *odora* 'Aureomarginata'		upright	○ to ◐	ordinary
ERICA *carnea* and varieties	ling, heather	hummock	○ to ◐	lime-tolerant
GARRYA *elliptica*	silk-tassel bush	upright spreading	◐ to ●	well-drained
HEBE: see Plants for Window Boxes				

Height/Spread		D/E	Foliage	Flower	Fruit	Comments
ft	8 ft	E	spiny seagreen	soft yellow April/May	blue-black berries July/Nov	
ft	4 ft	E	bright green, felty on underside	white, fragrant July		sunny site backed by wall
ft	8 ft	E	bright green	blue Aug/Oct		
ft	8 ft	E	bright green	deep blue May/June		
t	5 ft	E	glossy aromatic	white, fragrant May/June		successful against wall
3 ft	2–3 ft	E	dark to rich green	white to crimson and purple June/July		slightly tender
ft	12 ft	E	shiny green	brilliant red claws May/June		'must' for any warm sheltered sit
ries		E	bright green, glaucous, gold, purple			
t	3 ft	E	silver silky texture	pinky-white May/June		
ft	8 ft	E	grey leathery		red berries Oct/March	
ft	6 ft	E	bright green	white June/Aug	crimson berries Oct/Feb	
	10 ft	E	reddish in autumn		bright red berries Oct/March	
t	5 ft	E	dark shiny holly-like	scarlet tipped yellow July/Sep		sheltered position
		E	bright green, creamy margin	reddish purple Feb/March		sheltered position
	1½ ft	E	dark green to gold	white to purplish Nov/March		
	6 ft	E	grey-green	silky catkins Jan/Feb		wall shrub for south and south-west aspects

Botanical Name	Common Name	Habit	Sun/Shade	Soil
HYPERICUM *calycinum*	St. John's wort or rose of Sharon	spreading	○ to ◑	ordinary well-drained
moserianum 'Tricolor'		spreading	○ to ◑	ordinary well-drained
LAVANDULA all species and varieties	lavender	bushy	○	well-drained

MAHONIA: see Trees and Shrubs for Shade and Trees Shrubs for Winter Colour

MAGNOLIA *delavayi*		spreading bushy tree	○ to ◑	rich sandy
grandiflora		rounded shrub or bushy tree	○ to ◑	rich sandy
MYRTUS *communis*	myrtle	spreading	◑	well-drained
OLEARIA all species	daisy bush	rounded to spreading	○ to ◑	well-drained good on cha
PERNETTYA *mucronata* varieties	prickly heath	spreading wiry bush	◑ to ●	lime-free

RHODODENDRON: see Plants for Acid Soils

ROSMARINUS *officinalis*	rosemary	upright spreading	○	light
SENECIO *greyi*		spreading	○	well-drained
VIBURNUM *davidii*		hummock	◑ to ●	any
rhytidophyllum		upright, spreading	◑ to ●	any
tinus	laurustinus	spreading	○ to ◑	any

CLIMBING SHRUBS

BERBERIDOPSIS *corallina*	coral plant	straggly climber	◑	sandy
CISSUS *striata*		spreading climber	◑	rich peaty
CLEMATIS *cirrhosa balearica*	fern-leaved clematis	twining climber	○ to ◑	rich well-drained

ght/Spread		D/E	Foliage	Flower	Fruit	Comments
		E	rich green	bright yellow June/Aug		*will spread as far as allowed
t	3 ft	E	variegated pink, green, white	yellow June/Sep		needs shelter
ft	1½–3 ft	E	grey	pale blue to deep purple May/Aug		
o ft	15 ft	E	sea green, very large	creamy white, fragrant Aug/Sep		tender
t	6 ft	E	glossy green	pure white, fragrant July/Aug		excellent wall shrub
	2 ft	E	dark, glossy, aromatic	white July/Aug	purplish black Sep/Nov	some protection needed
ft	4 ft	E	grey-green to downy	white, fragrant July/Sep		very wind resistant
	3 ft	E	small shiny green	white	white to shiny dark red berries Nov/March	male and female plants for berries
	5 ft	E	grey-green, aromatic	bluish-lilac May/June		
t	3 ft	E	oval, grey-green, woolly	yellow daisies June/Aug		
	3 ft	E	dark green, corrugated	white May/July	turquoise berries on female form	male and female plants for berries
o ft	6–8 ft	E	large, dark green, felty	cream May/June	red berries Sept/Nov	
	6 ft	E	dark green	white Oct/March	blue berries Jan/June	
t	3 ft	E	glossy green, toothed	rich red July		warm wall
t	10 ft	E	dark glossy green			warm wall
t		E	pigmented bronzed in winter	pale yellow, spotted purple Jan/March		warm wall

Botanical Name	Common Name	Habit	Sun/Shade	Soil
armandii		twining climber	○ to ◑	rich well-draine
ESCALLONIA most species and varieties		upright spreading	○ to ◑	well-draine
HEDERA: see Plants for Shade				
PYRACANTHA: see Plants for Winter Colour				

SMAl

Botanical Name	Common Name	Habit	Sun/Shade	Soil
ACER *griseum*	paperbark maple	open small tree	○	moist well-draine
ACER *palmatum* 'Senkaki'	coral bark maple	open shrub or tree	○	moist well-draine
AMELANCHIER *lamarckii*	snowy Mespilias	round headed tree	○	ordinary
AZARA *microphylla*		bushy tree	○	ordinary
BETULA *pendula*	silver birch	slender, pendular	○	ordinary moist
pendula 'Tristis'		narrow, symmetrical	○	ordinary moist
pendula 'Youngii'	Young's weeping birch	rounded	○	ordinary moist
CATALPA *bignonioides*	Indian bean tree	rounded head	○	rich moist
CERCIS *siliquastrum*	Judas tree	rounded	○ to ◑	rich sandy
CHAMAECYPARIS *lawsoniana* 'Nana'		rounded conifer	○	rich
lawsoniana 'Stewartii'		conical conifer	○	rich sandy
COTONEASTER good varieties: *frigidus*, *salicifolius* 'Autumn Fire', *wardii*		broad head standard	○ to ◑	ordinary
CYTISUS *battandieri*	Moroccan broom	standard, has to be trained	○	sandy

ight/Spread		D/E	Foliage	Flower	Fruit	Comments
ft		E	leathery dark green	ivory white March/April		
×2 ft	6–8 ft	E	bright green	white, pink, red July/Sep		avoid east wall

REES

ight/Spread		D/E	Foliage	Flower	Fruit	Comments
ft	15 ft	D	deep scarlet in autumn			flaky paper bark
·15 ft	8 ft	D	canary yellow in autumn			branches coral red
ft	12 ft	D	rich reds in autumn	white March/April	red berries June/July	
ft	10 ft	E		yellow, scented May/April		only hardy in south
ft +	8–10 ft	D	rich yellow autumn			silver bark
·30 ft	6–8 ft	D	rich yellow autumn			yellowish bark
·15 ft	8–10 ft	D	rich yellow autumn			silver bark, needs careful training
t +	10–15 ft	D	large, in form 'Aurea'	white flecked yellow July/Aug	large beans Sep/Dec	
20 ft	12–15 ft	D	large deep green	purple April	purplish pods July on	
	2 ft	E	rich green			slow growing
t +	4–5 ft	E	bright yellow			
15 ft	6–8 ft	E	reddish tinges in autumn	white May/July— depending on variety	orange to red berries	
12 ft	6–8 ft	D	silky	bright yellow scented June/July		only completely hardy in south

Botanical Name	Common Name	Habit	Sun/Shade	Soil
DAVIDIA *vilmoriniana involuerata*	ghost, handkerchief, or Chinese dove tree	spreading	○	rich
EUCRYPHIA *glutinosa*		erect branching	○ to ◑	light rich
GINKGO *biloba*	maidenhair tree	columnar	○	light
LABURNUM *anagyroides*	golden rain common laburnum	spreading	○ to ◑	ordinary
alpinum	Scottish laburnum	spreading	○ to ◑	ordinary
× *watereri vossii*		spreading semi-sweeping	○ to ◑	ordinary
MAGNOLIA *soulangiana* varieties		spreading	○	rich sandy
stellata		spreading	○	rich sandy
MALUS × *robusta*	crab apple	broad head	○	ordinary
'Veitch's Scarlet'		compact	○	ordinary
PINUS *mugo*	mountain pine	bushy	○	rich
PRUNUS	flowering cherry	bushes standards standard weeping	○ ○ ○	ordinary ordinary ordinary
PYRUS *salicifolia* 'Pendula'	willow-leaved pear	weeping	○	ordinary
RHODODENDRONS (preferably grow as shrubs): see Plants for Acid Soils				
SOPHORA *japonica*	Japanese pagoda tree	rounded	○	rich sandy
SORBUS *scopulina*		erect branched	○	ordinary well-drain
cashmiriana		rounded	○	ordinary well-drain
TSUGA *canadensis* 'Pendula'	weeping eastern hemlock	spreading weeping conifer	○	deep rich

ght/Spread	D/E	Foliage	Flower	Fruit	Comments
20 ft 10–15 ft	D	bright green	white May		will not flower until about 8 years old
18 ft 7–10 ft	D	reddish tints autumn	white July/Aug		
25 ft 6–7 ft	D	rich yellow autumn			
23 ft 10–15 ft	D		yellow April/May		
20 ft 10–12 ft	D		yellow June		
18 ft 10–12 ft	D		yellow June		
2 ft 6–12 ft	D	dull green	creamy white to purple April/May		
ft 6–8 ft	D		white March/April		
25 ft 15 ft	D	reddish tints autumn		red or yellow fruits Oct/Dec	
15 ft 7–10 ft	D	reddish-browns, autumn	white	red berries	
15 ft 8–12 ft	E	rigid, curved leaves		cones	
2 ft 6–8 ft 25 ft 10–18 ft 15 ft 10–12 ft	D D D	most have rich autumn tints	white to deep rose March/June		weeping types make best trees for small gardens
18 ft 10–15 ft	D	silky white to grey-green	white April/May		
25 ft 10–15 ft	D		white Sep		
6–7 ft	D			deep red Sep/Nov	slow growing
20 ft 12–15 ft	D	white tinted pink May		large white Aug/Nov	
10 ft	E	green and white			very slow growing

TREES AND SHRUBS

Botanical Name	Common Name	Habit	Sun/Shade	Soil
BUDDLEIA *alternifolia*	butterfly bush	spreading, arching	○	light
davidii and varieties		upright, spreading	○ to ◑	light
globosa	orange ball tree	upright, spreading	○ to ◑	light
CISTUS all species	rock rose	hummock	○	light poor
CYTISUS all species	broom	rounded compact to upright spreading	○	sandy
GENISTA *hispanica*	Spanish gorse	spreading	○	ordinary well-draine
aetnensis	Mount Etna broom	pendulous	○	ordinary well-draine
HIBISCUS *syriacus* all varieties	mallow or shrubby Althaea	upright spreading	○	rich light
HYPERICUM *calcyinum*	rose of Sharon	spreading	○ to ◑	ordinary well-draine
LAVANDULA all species and varieties	lavender	bushy	○	well-draine
LIPPIA *citriodora*	lemon-scented verbena	open bush	○	light
OLEARIA × *scilloniensis*	daisy bush	rounded compact	○	any
PHLOMIS *fruticosa*	Jerusalem sage	upright	○	well-draine
POTENTILLA *fruticosa* and varieties	cinquefoil	bushy to prostrate	○ to ◑	any
ROSMARINUS *officinalis*	rosemary	spreading	○	well-draine
PUNICA *granatum*	pomegranate	upright spreading	○	well-draine
SENECIO *greyi*		spreading	○	well-draine

ht/Spread		D/E	Foliage	Flower	Fruit	Comments
	6 ft	D		soft lilac, fragrant May		
	7 ft	D	greyish-green	pure white to deep purple July/Aug		
	8 ft	D	dark green	yellow, scented June		
ft	3 ft	E	dark to rich green	white to crimson June/Aug		
t	3–7 ft	D		white, yellow and purple —often bicolour June/July		
	4 ft	D		golden yellow May/June		
	8 ft	D		golden yellow July		
	6 ft	D		white blue to deep maroon Aug/Sep		
	3 ft	E	rich green	bright yellow June/Aug		
t	1½–3 ft	E	grey	pale blue to deep purple May/Aug		
	3 ft	D	scented	mauve Aug		prefers warm wall
t	3 ft	E	grey	white May/June		
	4 ft	E	grey-green	bright yellow June/July		
t	3–5 ft	D		primrose yellow to orange June/Aug		
	5 ft	E	grey	bluish-mauve, scented May/June		
	3 ft	(S)	reddish tinges in autumn	scarlet June/Aug		prefers warm wall
	3 ft	E	grey-green woolly	yellow daisies June/Aug		

Botanical Name	Common Name	Habit	Sun/Shade	Soil
SPARTIUM *junceum*	Spanish broom	upright spreading	○ to ◐	light
YUCCA *gloriosa*	Adam's needle	small spreading tree	○	ordinary well-drain

HERBACEOUS—HARDY BULBS

Botanical Name	Common Name	Habit	Sun/Shade	Soil
ANAPHALIS *triplinervis*		upright spreading	○	ordinary
ANTHEMIS *tinctoria*	dyer's or ox-eye chamomile	cushion	○	ordinary
ARMERIA all species	thrift	dense cushion	○	well-drain
CENTRANTHUS *rubra*	red valerian	upright spreading	○	well-drain
DIANTHUS all varieties	pinks	carpet	○	rich well-drain
ECHINOPS *humilis* 'Taplow Blue'	globe thistle	upright	○	ordinary
ERYNGIUM *tripartitum*	sea holly	spreading	○	sandy
variifolium		spreading	○	sandy
HELIANTHEMUM all varieties	sun rose	spreading	○	ordinary
LINUM *perenne*	flax	upright	○	well-drain
LUPINUS Russell varieties	lupin	upright spreading	○	light
NEPETA *gigantea* or 'Six Hills Giant'	catmint	clump	○	ordinary
PAPAVER *orientalis* varieties	Oriental poppy	upright	○	light
SEDUM all species and varieties	stonecrop	cushion spreader	○	ordinary

ght/Spread		D/E	Foliage	Flower	Fruit	Comments
	5 ft	D		yellow June/Sep		
	6 ft	E	long narrow pointed	creamy white July/Sep		spasmodic flowerer
½ ft		D	woolly	white, everlasting Aug/Sep		
½ ft		E	silvery grey	yellow June/Aug		
ɔ in		E		pinks May/June		
		E		scarlet June/Sep		
₂ in	2–3 ft	E	grey	white, pink to reds June/July		ideal for edging
	3 ft	D	silvery grey	bright blue, everlasting July/Aug		
₹	3½ ft	E	jagged margin, steely tinge	steel blue June/Aug		} leaves form tight rosettes in winter
₹	2 ft	E	steely green with conspicuous white veins	whitish green June/Aug		
	1–1½ ft	E	silvery grey	primrose to warm browns May/July		ideal for dry walls
		D		pale blue June		
		D		all colours except blue May/Aug		
½ ft	2½–3 ft	(S)	grey-green woolly	lavender blue June/Aug		
₃ ft		D	pale green	white and pink to crimson May/June		
–2 ft		D	fleshy, often tinged purple or glaucous	yellow, pinks to crimson July/Oct		small species ideal for dry walls

Botanical Name	Common Name	Habit	Sun/Shade	Soil
SEMPERVIVUM	houseleek	carpeting	○	well-drain◄
VERBASCUM all species	mullein	upright	○	well-drain◄

SEASONAL PLANTING

Botanical Name	Common Name	Habit	Sun/Shade	Soil
CENTAUREA *cyanus* all varieties	cornflower	upright	○	ordinary
DIMORPHOTHECA all species and varieties	star of the veldt or Cape marigold	spreading	○	light
ESCHSCHOLZIA	Californian poppy	spreading	○	light
GAZANIA varieties	treasure flower	spreading	○	light sandy
MESEMBRYANTHEMUM *criniflorum*	Livingstone daisy	spreading	○	light sandy
PELARGONIUM zonal scented ivy leaf	geraniums	bushy to spreading trailing	○ to ◑	rich except for scented pelargoniu◄
PETUNIA all varieties		spreading	○ to ◑	ordinary
PORTULACA all varieties	purslane	upright	○	ordinary
URSINIA all species and varieties		spreading	○	ordinary

FO

TREES AND SHRUBS

Botanical Name	Common Name	Habit	Sun/Shade	Soil
ARUNDINARIA *japonica*	bamboo	upright clump	◑ to ●	all but heavy clay
nitida	bamboo	upright clump	◑ to ●	all but heavy clay◄
variegata	variegated bamboo	upright tufted	◑ to ●	all but heavy clay◄

ght/Spread		D/E	Foliage	Flower	Fruit	Comments
		E	succulent tight rosettes	purplish to pale yellow June/Aug		many varieties ideal for rockeries and walls
ft		D	thick woolly	golden yellows June/July		
½ ft			spiky, often silvery green	pale blue to deep scarlets June/Sep		sow seed direct, March on
–1 ft				white to deep orange May/Sep		sow seed direct April on; flower 6 wks. from sowing
n				all colours June/Sep		sow seed direct April on
15 in		E		yellow, pink to scarlet July/Oct		plant June
	15 in		glaucous fleshy	pink to rich orange July/Sep		plant June
ft	1–2 ft	E	greens, purples, whites, often textured	white to mauves and deep purples May/Oct		plant May/June
½ ft	1 ft		soft green	white to reds and blues June/Sep		plant May/June
2 in	1½ ft		edible	all colours June/Sep		sow seeds April/May
15 in				bright yellow to orange June/Sep		sow seed April

IADE

ght/Spread		D/E	Foliage	Flower	Fruit	Comments
t	varies	E	lush glossy green			thickets of olive-green canes
t	varies	E	thin delicate pale green			ideal for containers
ft	varies	E	dark green white stripes			zigzag pale green canes; ideal for containers

Botanical Name	Common Name	Habit	Sun/Shade	Soil
AUCUBA *japonica* 'Variegata'		rounded	◑ to ●	any
AZALEAS: see under Rhododendron in Plants for Acid Soils				
CAMELLIA: see Plants for Acid Soils				
MAHONIA *aquifolium*	Oregon grape	upright spreading shrub	◑ to ●	any
'Charity'		upright	◑ to ●	moist
japonica		upright	◑ to ●	moist
PIERIS *formosa forrestii*		large rounded	◑ to ●	peaty well-drained
RHODODENDRONS: see Plants for Acid Soils				
RUSCUS *aculeatus*	butcher's broom	erect clump	○ to ●	light
SARCOCOCCA *humilis*	sweet box	hummock	◑ to ●	any
SKIMMIA *japonica*		hummock	○ to ◑	acid
VINCA *major*	large periwinkle	carpet rooting	◑ to ●	any
minor	lesser periwinkle	carpet rooting	◑ to ●	any

HERBACEOUS—HARDY BULBS

Botanical Name	Common Name	Habit	Sun/Shade	Soil
ACONITUM 'Blue Sceptre'	monkshood	upright clump	◑	ordinary
ANEMONE *hupehensis japonica*	Japanese anemone	erect spreading	○ to ●	peaty
elegans 'Honorine Jobert'	white Japanese anemone	erect spreading	◑ to ●	peaty
ASTRANTIA *major*	masterwort	erect spreading	◑	cool position
CONVALLARIA *majalis*	lily-of-the-valley	spreading	○ to ●	well-drained
CYCLAMEN *neapolitanum*		tuberous spreading	◑ to ●	rich loam

ght/Spread	D/E	Foliage	Flower	Fruit	Comments
4 ft	E	glossy green speckled yellow	inconspicuous	red berries on female Oct/March	one of the most hardy shrubs
3 ft	E	shiny dark green pinnate	yellow clusters March/May		
4 ft	E	large shiny dark green pinnate	large racemes, deep yellow Nov/Jan		architectural plant
4 ft	E	shiny dark green pinnate	yellow racemes Oct/Feb	blue berries Jan/March	
5 ft	E	brilliant red in spring	white panicles April/May		some protection in north
2 ft	E	stiff, spiny dark green	greenish May	red berries Sep on	
3 ft	E	small bluish-green	white, scented Feb		suitable for under dense trees
3 ft	E	glossy green, aromatic	white April/May	red berries Oct/March	male and female forms for berries
2 ft	E	glossy green	bright blue May/Oct		ground cover for any site
1½ ft	E	glossy green	blue June/Aug		ground cover for any site
2½ ft	D	large palmate	blue and white July/Aug		very poisonous
2 ft	D	large palmate	semi-double rose Aug/Oct		suitable for under trees
2 ft	D	large palmate	white Aug/Oct		suitable for under trees
2 ft	D	large lobed	green tinged white June/July		shade by pool
1½ ft	D	smooth rich green	white bells, scented April/May		needs time to settle
10 in	(S)	velvety green, white markings	rosy-pink Aug/Oct		suitable for under trees

Botanical Name	Common Name	Habit	Sun/Shade	Soil
ENDYMION *nonscriptus*	English bluebell	bulbous spreading	◐ to ●	lime-free
ERANTHIS *hyemalis*	winter aconite	tuberous spreading	◐ to ●	not alkaline
GALANTHUS *nivalis*	snowdrop	bulbous spreader	○ to ●	ordinary
HELLEBORUS *foetidus*		clump	◐ to ●	moist rich loam
nigra	Christmas rose	clump	○ to ●	moist rich loam

HERBACEOUS

HOSTA *crispula*	plantain lily	spreader	○ to ●	lime-free
fortunei		clump	◐ to ●	lime-free
fortunei albo-picta		clump	◐	lime-free
lancifolia		clump	◐ to ●	lime-free
POLYGONATUM *multiflorum*	Solomon's seal	erect spreading	◐ to ●	moist, lime-free
PRIMULA *denticulata*	drumstick primrose	clump	◐	moist, heavy
japonica varieties	Japanese primrose	clump	◐	moist, heavy
'Polyanthus'	polyanthus	clump	◐	moist, heavy
veris	cowslip	clump	◐ to ●	moist, heavy
SAXIFRAGA *umbrosa*	London pride	spreading	○ to ●	moist
TIARELLA *cordifolia*	foam flower	carpet rooting	◐ to ●	cool, well-draine
VIOLA *cornuta*	horned violet	carpet rooting	◐ to ●	moist, well-draine
cornuta 'Alba'	white horned violet	carpet rooting	◐ to ●	moist, well-draine

ght/Spread	D/E	Foliage	Flower	Fruit	Comments
in	D	lush green	blue April		
10 in	D	bright green	yellow Jan/Feb		suitable for under trees
	D	rich green	white Jan/Feb		many varieties with larger flowers
	E	large dark green	citron Feb/April		
	E	large dark green	white Nov/Feb		
1½ ft	D	dark broad green, white margin	pale lilac July/Aug		
3 ft	D	large broad, glaucous green	pale lilac July/Aug		
1 ft	D	broad green and yellow	lilac July		
1 ft	D	narrow, dark green	lilac Aug/Sep		
1 ft	D	long, broad	greenish-yellow bells April/May		
1 ft	(S)	soft green rosette	white, lilac, crimson March/May		globular flower heads
1 ft	(S)	rosette	white, pink, crimson May/July		
1 ft	(S)	rosette	many colours March/May		many hybrids ideal for spring bedding
9 in	(S)	soft green rosette	golden yellow April/May		
9 in	E	purplish-green rosettes	pink April/May		excellent ground cover
1½ ft	D	heart-shaped	fluffy white April/May		prolific ground cover
1½ ft	E	lush light green	lilac-purple May/June and Aug/Sep		
1 ft	E	lush light green	white May/June and Aug/Sep		

CLIMBING SHRUBS

Botanical Name	Common Name	Habit	Sun/Shade	Soil
HEDERA *canariensis* 'Variegata'	Canary Island ivy	matty climber	○ to ◕	well-drain
colchica	Persian ivy	matty climber	◑ to ◕	any
colchica 'Paddy's Pride'		matty climber	○ to ◕	any
helix	common ivy	matty climber	◑ to ◕	any
helix 'Buttercup'		matty climber	○ to ◕	any

Note: all are excellent self-supporting climbers for walls.

FERNS: see Plants for Acid Soils

FOR ACI

TREES AND SHRUBS

Botanical Name	Common Name	Habit	Sun/Shade	Soil
AZALEA: see under Rhododendron				
BETULA *pendula*	silver birch	slender weeping tree	○	does well on poor s•
CALLUNA *vulgaris*	heather or ling	hummock	○ to ◑	peaty
CAMELLIA *japonica* 'Adophe Audusson'		compact rounded	◑ to ◉	moist, ric in humus
japonica 'Mathotiana Alba'		loose rounded	◑ to ◕	moist, ric in humus
japonica 'Mathotiana Rosea'		compact rounded	◑ to ◉	moist, ric in humus
× *williamsii* 'Donation'		rounded open	◑ to ◕	moist, ric in humus
CRINODENDRON *hookerianum*		upright dense	◑	moist peaty
DABOECIA *cantabrica*	Irish heath	loose hummock	○ to ◑	rich peaty
DAPHNE *collina neapolitana*		upright	○ to ◑	ordinary
ENKIANTHUS *campanulatus*		erect spreading	◑	peaty

t/Spread	D/E	Foliage	Flower	Fruit	Comments
12 ft	E	large, dark green white margin			avoid east and north-east aspects
15 ft	E	large dark green leathery			
12 ft	E	large dark green splashed with yellow			
10 ft	E	small dark glossy green			excellent ground cover
6 ft	E	small bright yellow			best golden form

OILS

t/Spread	D/E	Foliage	Flower	Fruit	Comments
10 ft	D	golden yellow in autumn			provides modest shade
2 ft	E	small grey-green	purplish July/Sep		many varieties
5 ft	E	bold glossy green	blood red semi-double March/May		
5 ft	E	bold glossy green	white double March/April		slightly tender
5 ft	E	bold glossy green	pink double March/April		slightly tender
5 ft	E	bold glossy green	pink semi-double Feb/May		
9 ft	E		hanging crimson lanterns May		tender, north walls in south only
2 ft	E	small rich green	rose-purple June/Nov		many good varieties
	E	ash green	rose-pink, fragrant April/June		
4 ft	D	orange-yellow to red in autumn	pale cream veined red May		

F

Botanical Name	Common Name	Habit	Sun/Shade	Soil
ERICA all species	heath	hummock	○ to ◐	peaty
EUCRYPHIA × *nymansensis*		upright	○ to ◐	lime-tolerant
FOTHERGILLA *monticola*	American witch hazel	upright spreader	○ to ◐	well-drain sandy pea
GAULTHERIA *procumbens*	partridge berry	spreader	○ to ◐	drought-tolerant
KALMIA *latifolia*	calico bush	rounded dense	◐	ordinary
LITHOSPERMUM *diffusum*	gromwell	prostrate spreading	○	sandy
MENZIESIA *ciliicalyx*		rounded	○ to ◐	peaty
NYSSA *sylvatica*	tupelo	broadly columnar tree or large shrub		moist
PERNETTYA *mucronata*	prickly heath	dense wiry thickets	◐ to ●	peaty
PHILESIA *magellanica*		broad wiry thicket	◐	moist peaty
PHYLLODOCE × *intermedia*		large mats	○	cool sandy pea
PIERIS *formosa forrestii*		large rounded shrub	◐ to ●	peaty

RHODODENDRON SPECIES and HYBRIDS including AZALEAS

'Britannia'		rounded shrub	◐	peaty
discolor		upright spreader	◐	peaty
forrestii repens		hummock	◐	peaty
luteum		upright spreader	○ to ◐	peaty
'Pink Pearl'		rounded bush	◐	peaty
'Sapphire'		cushion		peaty

/Spread	D/E	Foliage	Flower	Fruit	Comments
1–3 ft	E	small, green, purple to gold	white to purple		flowering season depends on specie
3 ft	E	dark shining green	white, scented Aug		excellent ground cover
3 ft	D	rich autumn colours	white, scented May		
1½ ft	E	dark glossy green	tiny white bells June/Aug	scarlet fruits Sep/Feb	
5 ft	E	large glossy green	pink June		slightly tender
1½ ft	E	dull green hairy	blue April/June		dry hot corners
3 ft	D		crimson to soft purple May		very beautiful
10 ft– 15 ft	D	rich scarlet in autumn			
3½ ft	E	dark green prickly	white	purplish berries Oct/March	male and female for berries
3 ft	E	narrow rigid	crimson July/Sep		sheltered site
4 ft	E		reddish-purple April/May		very vigorous
5 ft		brilliant red in spring	white panicles April/May		some protection in north
5 ft	E	large glossy green	crimson trumpet-shaped May/June		very wind resistant
5 ft	E		pink and yellow scented		
3 ft	E	glaucous green	scarlet bell-shaped April/May		very choice ground cover
4 ft	D	bright reddish yellows autumn	orange-yellow scented May/June		
ft 7 ft	E	large glossy green	deep lilac-pink June/July		
3 ft	E	bluish green	clear blue April/May		

163

Botanical Name	Common Name	Habit	Sun/Shade	Soil
'Yellow Hammer'		upright	◐	peaty
DECIDUOUS AZALEAS 'Bouquet de Flore'		bushy	○ to ◐	peaty
'Fireglow'		bushy	○ to ◐	peaty
'Persil'		bushy	○ to ◐	peaty
'Satan'		bushy	○ to ◐	peaty
'W. S. Churchill'		cushion	○ to ◐	peaty
EVERGREEN AZALEAS 'Adonis'		cushion	◐	peaty
'Blue Danube'		cushion	◐	peaty
'Helena'		cushion	◐	peaty
'Orange Beauty'		cushion	◐	peaty
'Vuyk's Scarlet'		cushion	◐	peaty
VACCINIUM *macrocarpum*	American cranberry	carpet rooting	○ to ●	tolerant extreme acidity

CLIMBING SHRUBS

BERBERIDOPSIS *corallina*	coral plant	straggly climber	◐	sandy
LAPAGERIA *rosea*	Chilean bellflower	wiry climber	◐ to ●	peaty

HERBACEOUS—HARDY BULBS

GENTIANA *asclepiadea*	willow gentian	upright	◐	moist
lutea	yellow gentian	upright	◐	moist

t/Spread	D/E	Foliage	Flower	Fruit	Comments
3 ft	E		yellow bell-shaped March/April		often flowers again in autumn
5–6 ft	D	reddish hue autumn	salmon-pink scented May		
4 ft	D	reddish hue autumn	orange, scented May		
4 ft	D	reddish hue in autumn	white and yellow, scented		
4 ft	D	reddish hue in autumn	geranium red, scented May		
4 ft	D	reddish hue in autumn	red blotched, scented May		
3½ ft	E		pink double May		all successful in containers but slightly tender in east and north-east aspects
3½ ft	E		bluish-violet May		
3½ ft	E		large white May		
3½ ft	E		orange-pink May		
3½ ft	E		bright red May		
3 ft	E	tight mat	pinkish-reddish white June/Aug Sep/Feb		
3 ft	E	glossy green	blood-red clusters July/Sep		north or west aspect
4 ft	E	stiff, leathery	pink, fleshy, bell-shaped July/Aug		need shelter of west wall; southern counties only
1½ ft	(S)		azure July/Aug		plant near pools
2 ft	(S)		yellow July/Aug		

HERBACEOUS

Botanical Name	Common Name	Habit	Sun/Shade	Soil
LILIUM *aurelianense*		erect	○ to ◐	well-drai
candidum	Madonna lily	erect	○	well-drai
martagon	common Turk's Cap lily	erect	◐	well-drai
regale		erect	○	well-drai
tigrinum	tiger lily	erect	○	well-drai
SEDUM 'Ruby Glow'	stonecrop	cushion spreader	○ to ◐	tolerant t dry soils
spectabile 'Brilliant'	ice plant	cushion spreader	○ to ◐	tolerant t dry soils
THYMUS *serpyllum*	wild thyme	prostrate mat	○ to ◐	light

FERNS

Botanical Name	Common Name	Habit	Sun/Shade	Soil
ADIANTUM *pedatum*	North American maidenhair fern	clump	◐ to ●	moist well-drai
BLECHNUM *spicant*	hard fern	tufted	◐ to ●	moist well-drai
DRYOPTERIS *filix-mas*	male fern	clump	○ to ●	tolerant t dry soils
OSMUNDA *regalis*	Royal fern	clump	◐ to ●	very moi

FOR CHAL

TREES AND SHRUBS

Botanical Name	Common Name	Habit	Sun/Shade	Soil
ABELIA *floribunda*		rounded	○	chalky-loam
× *grandiflora*		rounded	○	chalky-loam
ACER *campestre*	hedge or field maple	rounded	○	moist well-drai
pseudo-platanus 'Nizettii'		rounded	○	moist well-drai

ht/Spread		D/E	Foliage	Flower	Fruit	Comments
ft		D		whitish and yellow Aug		plant bulbs 9 in deep
ft		D		white June/July		plant bulbs 6 in deep
		D		rosy-purple		plant bulbs 4 in deep
ft		D		July white with yellow and purple July		tender in north plant bulbs 9 in deep
ft		D		orange-red spotted purple Aug/Sep		plant bulbs 6 in deep
	15 in	(S)	purplish-grey, fleshy	ruby-red July/Sep		many other excellent species
	3 ft	(S)	pale-grey, fleshy	bright pink Sep/Oct		many other excellent species
	9 in	E	woolly grey, aromatic	mauve June/July		a must for the herb garden

ft	1 ft	D	soft green, dainty			
	1 ft	D	bright green			
t	2 ft	D	dull green			most hardy fern
ft	3 ft	D	fresh green, large	brown fertile fronds July/Sep		perfect in shade near ponds

OILS

ht/Spread		D/E	Foliage	Flower	Fruit	Comments
	5 ft	(S)	glossy green	cherry red, tubular June		against warm wall
	4 ft	(S)	brilliant dark green	pink and white July/Sep		
	15 ft	D	gold and red autumn			
	10–12 ft	D	golden to white tinted pink			

Botanical Name	Common Name	Habit	Sun/Shade	Soil
BERBERIS all species and varieties		usually dense rounded bushes	◐ to ●	ordinary
BETULA (Birch): see Small Trees				
BUXUS *sempervirens* and varieties	common box	compact rounded clump	◐ to ●	any
CHIMONANTHUS *praecox*	wintersweet	upright spreading shrub	○ to ◐	well-drain
COTINUS *coggyria* and varieties	Venetian sumach, smoke tree	upright spreading	◐	sandy
typhina	stag's horn sumach	upright	○ to ◐	sandy
COTONEASTER (Standard): see Small Trees COTONEASTER (Shrubs): see Shrubs for All Year Round Foliage all species and varieties DAPHNE MEZEREUM: see Trees and Shrubs for Winter Colour				
DEUTZIA × *elegantissima*		upright arching	○ to ◐	ordinary well-drain
'Magician'		upright	○ to ◐	
scabra		upright arching	○ to ◐	
ESCALLONIA all varieties following are very good 'C. F. Ball'		upright spreading	○ to ◐	rich
'Donard Star'		compact upright	○ to ◐	rich
'Iveyi'		upright spreading	○ to ◐	rich
'Slieve Donard'		upright	○ to ◐	rich
FORSYTHIA 'Arnold Dwarf'	golden bell bush	spreading	○ to ◐	any
'Beatrix Farrand'		upright	○ to ◐	any
ovata		rounded	○ to ◐	any
viridissima 'Bronxensis'		compact, dwarf	○ to ◐	any

ht/Spread		D/E	Foliage	Flower	Fruit	Comments
ft	5–12 ft	D and E	varies greatly usually very spiny	yellows and reds, mainly April/July	red, blue or purple berries	
	3 ft	2 E	dark green, golden or variegated			
	4 ft	D	bright green	pale yellow Jan/Feb		wall shrub
ft	5 ft +	D	reds and yellows autumn	pink July/Aug		
	8 ft	D	reds and yellows autumn		females show pink fruits Aug/Sep	
ft	4 ft	D		rose pink April/May		
	4 ft	D		mauvish-pink, scented May/June		
	4 ft	D		white April/May		
	5 ft	E	dark green	deep red Aug/Sep		
ft	5 ft	E		rose pink July/Sep		all are good wall shrubs
ft	4–5 ft	E		white July/Sep		
ft	5 ft	E		peach-pink Aug/Sep		
ft	6 ft	D		yellow green March/April		
	5 ft	D		yellow March/April		
	4 ft	D		amber yellow Feb/March		
	3 ft	D		lemon yellow April		

F*

Botanical Name	Common Name	Habit	Sun/Shade	Soil
FUCHSIA all varieties and species		open bushes	○ to ◑	ordinary
GARRYA *elliptica*	silk-tassel bush	upright spreading	◑ to ●	ordinary well-drained
GENISTA *aetnensis*	Spanish gorse	spreading	○	ordinary well-drained
hispanica	Mount Etna broom	pendulous	○	ordinary well-drained
HEBE: see Plants for Window Boxes				
HIBISCUS *syriacus* all varieties	mallow or shrubby Althaea	upright spreading	○	rich light loam
JUNIPERUS *communis* 'Hibernica'	Irish juniper	dense pillar	○	light
virginiana 'Skyrocket'		columnar	○	light
LABURNUM: see Small Trees				
LAVANDULA *spica*	old English lavender	bushy	○	well-drained
spica 'Hidcote'		dense	○	well-drained
spica 'Vera'	Dutch lavender	dense	○	well-drained
OLEARIA: see Evergreens				
PAEONIA *delavayi*	tree paeony	spreading	◑	rich, heavy
lutea	tree paeony	spreading	◑	rich, heavy
PRUNUS (Japanese Cherries): see Small Trees				
RIBES *odoratum*	Buffalo currant	upright spreading	◑ to ●	ordinary
sanguineum and varieties	flowering currant	upright spreading	◑ to ●	ordinary
speciosum	fuchsia-flowered gooseberry	spreading	◑ to ●	ordinary
ROSA (Rose: most species and hybrids tolerant)				
SKIMMIA *japonica*: see Trees and Shrubs for Winter Colour				
SPIRAEA *japonica* varieties		cushion	○ to ◑	ordinary

t/Spread	D/E	Foliage	Flower	Fruit	Comments
3–4 ft	D		pinks, purples and violets June/Oct		plant June; can be trained as standards
6 ft	E	grey-green	silky catkins Jan/Feb		wall shrub for south and south-west aspects
4 ft	D		golden yellow May/June		
8 ft	D		golden yellow July		
6 ft	D		white, blue to deep maroon July/Sep		
ft 2 ft	E	silvery			ideal where there is very limited space
1–1½ ft	E	glaucous green			
3 ft	E	grey	greyish-blue June/Aug		
1½ ft	E	grey	deep purple, blue May/July		
2 ft	E	grey	pale blue June/Aug		
3 ft	D	large green compound	crimson April/May		some protection from spring frosts
4 ft	D	large green compound	yellow April/May		
4 ft	D	rich reds autumn	bright yellow April/May	black July/Aug	
5 ft	D	rich autumn colour	bright red April/May	black	
4 ft	D		rich red April	red	good wall shrub
					prefer rich soil
3–4 ft	D		pink, purple May/Sep		

171

TREES AND SHRUBS—*cont.*

Botanical Name	Common Name	Habit	Sun/Shade	Soil
SYRINGA compact varieties	lilac	upright compact	○ to ◑	ordinary
TAMARIX *gallica*	French tamarisk	upright spreading	○	any
pentandra and varieties		upright spreading	○	any

HERBACEOUS—HARDY BULBS

ALTHAEA all varieties and species	hollyhock	erect	○ to ◑	any
IRIS *germanica* varieties	bearded iris	upright	○	any but heavy and
pumila	dwarf bearded iris	clump	○	well-drain
unguicularis	Algerian iris	clump	○	well-drain
NERINE *bowdenii*		clump	○	rich, well-drained; tolerant of limey condition
PAEONIA all species and varieties	paeony	clumps	○	deep, rich
VERONICA *incana*		spreading	○ to ◑	ordinary
longifolia		upright spreading	○ to ◑	ordinary
prostrata		spreading	○ to ◑	ordinary

CLIMBING SHRUBS

CLEMATIS all species and varieties	Virgin's bower	twining climber	○ to ◑	well-drain
JASMINUM *nudiflorum*	winter jasmine	twining climber	○ to ◑	moist well-drain

ht/Spread		D/E	Foliage	Flower	Fruit	Comments
ft	4–5 ft	D		white, blue, mauves, purples May/June		
ft	4–5 ft	E	grey-green	pink July/Sep		
ft	6–7 ft	E	glaucous	pale pink, red, scented July/Sep		
ft	2–3 ft	D		white, yellows, rose red, mauves July/Sep		sow seed outdoor in April
·½ ft		D		all colours May/June		
in		D		pale yellows to violet March/May		
		E		lavender blue, scented Jan/Feb		poor soils for maximum flowering
		D		pink Sep		protection from November/April
ft	3–4 ft	D	large green compound	white to deep crimson June/July		
ft		D	silver	dark blue June/July		
ft		D		bluish-lilac Aug		
in		D		rich blue June		
·5 ft	8–15 ft	D some E		whites pinks, lilacs to deep purples May/Oct		very wide range of flower sizes
	5 ft	D		bright yellow Nov/March		avoid east aspect, has green winter stems

173

Botanical Name	Common Name	Habit	Sun/Shade	Soil
WISTERIA *sinensis*	Chinese wisteria	spreading climber	○	ordinar

FOR AUTUMN (

TREES AND SHRUBS

Botanical Name	Common Name	Habit	Sun/Shade	Soil
ACER *griseum*	paperbark maple	small tree	○	moist well-drair
palmatum 'Senkaki'	coral bark maple	large shrub or small tree	○	moist well-drair
CALLICARPA *bodinieri giraldii*		open	○	ordinary loam
CHAMAECYPARIS *lawsoniana* 'Lutea'		columnar conifer	○	well-drair
CHIMONANTHUS *praecox*	winter sweet	upright spreading	○ to ◑	well-drair
CORNUS *alba* 'Sibirica'	Westonbirt dogwood	erect	○ to ◕	ordinary
stolonifera 'Flaviramea'	green dogwood	erect	○ to ◕	ordinary
DAPHNE *mezereum*		erect	○ to ◑	moist lime-free
ERICA *carnea*	heath	hummock	○ to ◑	lime-tolerant
FATSIA *japonica*		erect spreading	◑ to ◕	avoid lim
GARRYA *ellipitica*	silk tassel bush	upright spreading	◑ to ◕	ordinary
HAMAMELIS *mollis*	witch hazel	upright spreading	○ to ◑	rich, moi
ILEX *aquifolium*	holly	upright	○ to ◕	any
KERRIA *japonica* 'Pleniflora'	Jew's mallow	upright spreading	◑ to ◕	any
LINDERA *benzoin*	spice bush	shrubby tree	○	lime-free

ght/Spread		D/E	Foliage	Flower	Fruit	Comments
t	15 ft	D	bright green	deep lilac May to June		very vigorous

INTER COLOUR

ght/Spread		D/E	Foliage	Flower	Fruit	Comments
t	15 ft	D	scarlet shades in autumn	not conspicuous		good bark colour
t	8 ft	D	yellow in autumn	not conspicuous		coral-red bark
	5 ft	D	pinkish-mauves in autumn	lilac-pink July/Aug	violet berries Dec/Feb	south aspect
30 ft	5–6 ft	E	golden yellow			specimen tree
	4 ft	D	bright green	pale yellow Jan/Feb		wall shrub
	4 ft	D	reddish in autumn	whitish July		red stems in winter
	4 ft	D	reddish in autumn	whitish July		yellow-green stems in winter
	3 ft	D		rose, scented Feb/March	scarlet poisonous berries May	thrives in chalky soil
in	1½ ft	E	small dark green	white, pinks to purples Nov/March		many good varieties
	6 ft	E	large green palmate	milky-white Oct/Nov		striking tropical appearance
	6 ft	E	oval grey-green	silky catkins Jan/Feb		wall shrub for south and south-west aspects
	8 ft	D	golden yellow autumn	yellow red Jan/Feb		
t	10 ft	E	shiny dark green	not conspicuous	red berries Oct/March	male and female plants for berries
ft	varies	D	bright green	double yellow May/June		bright green stems in winter
t	10 ft	D	yellow in autumn	sulphur yellow March	red berries June/Sep	aromatic

Botanical Name	Common Name	Habit	Sun/Shade	Soil
MAHONIA *bealei*		upright spreading	◑	peaty
MALUS × *robusta*	crab apple	broad tree	○	ordinary
'Veitch's Scarlet'		compact tree	○	ordinary
PARROTIA *persica*		large shrub or small tree	◑	ordinary
PERNETTYA *mucronata* varieties	prickly heath	spreading wiry	◑ to ●	lime-free
PRUNUS *subhirtella* 'Autumnalis'	autumn cherry	small tree	○	ordinary
RHODODENDRONS: see Plants for Acid Soils				
RUBUS *cockburnianus*		spreading erect	◑	any
SENECIO *greyi*, *S. laxifolius*		spreading	○	well-drained
SKIMMIA *japonica*		dome-shaped	○ to ◑	avoid lime
THUJA *orientalis* 'Juniperoides'		dwarf-rounded conifer	○	deep moist
occidentalis 'Rheingold'		dwarf-rounded conifer	○	deep moist
VIBURNUM *betulifolium*		upright, spreading	◑	deep moist
fragrans		upright	○ to ◑	any
tinus	laurustinus	spreading	○ to ●	any

CLIMBING SHRUBS

JASMINUM *nudiflorum*	winter jasmine	trailing climber	○ to ◑	moist, well-drained
LONICERA *japonica* 'Aureoreticulata'	honeysuckle	rambling climber	◑ to ●	ordinary
PARTHENOCISSUS *quinquefolia*	Virginia creeper	self-clinging vine	◑ to ●	any

Height/Spread		D/E	Foliage	Flower	Fruit	Comments
ft	3 ft	E	large glossy green pinnate	yellow, scented Nov/March		some protection
ft	12 ft	D	reddish tinges autumn	white May	red or yellow Oct/Dec	specimen tree
–18 ft	12 ft	D	reddish-brown autumn	white May	red Oct/Dec	outstanding crab
ft	12 ft	D	reds and gold autumn	red tufts Jan/March		
ft	3 ft	E	small shiny green		white to shiny dark red berries Nov/March	group several plants for berries
ft	12 ft	D		white clusters intermittently all winter		good for cut sprays
ft	6 ft	D	fern-like	small purple June/July	black Sep/Nov	long arching purplish-white stems
ft	3 ft	E	oval, grey-green, woolly	yellow daisies June/Aug		
ft	3 ft	E	glossy green aromatic	white April/May	red berries Nov/Feb	male and female for berries
ft	2 ft	E	greyish-green, purplish in autumn			not east or north-east aspects
ft	2½ ft	E	bright rusty gold			
ft	8 ft	D	large, beech-like		redcurrant-like fruits	young plants don't fruit freely
ft	5 ft	D		pale pink clusters Oct/Feb		
ft	6 ft	E	oval, dark green	white Oct/March	blue-black berries Jan/June	
ft	5 ft	D		bright yellow Nov/March		avoid east aspect, green stems
ft	15 ft	(S)	green with golden veins	yellow, scented June/Aug		ideal trellis climber
ft	20 ft	D	large, rich autumn colour			a superb climber for any aspect

Botanical Name	Common Name	Habit	Sun/Shade	Soil
PYRACANTHA *rogersiana* 'Flava'	firethorn	upright spreading	○ to ◐	ordinary well-drained
'Watereri'	firethorn	upright spreading	○ to ◐	ordinary well-drained
VITIS *coignetiæ*	vine	twining climber	○ to ◐	rich

HERBACEOUS

ERANTHIS *hyemalis*	winter aconite	tuberous spreader	◐ to ●	not alkaline
HELLEBORUS *nigra*	Christmas rose	clump	○ to ●	rich
IRIS *unguicularis*	Algerian iris	clump	○	light, well-drained
SEMPERVIVUM species	houseleek	carpeting	○	well-drained

Height/Spread		D/E	Foliage	Flower	Fruit	Comments
0 ft	12 ft	E		white April/May	yellow berries Oct/Feb	wall shrubs
ft	8 ft	E		white April/May	red berries Oct/Feb	good hedging plant
5 ft	varies	D	large, brilliant red in autumn	small clusters, scented June/July		spectacular
in	10 in	D	bright green	yellow Jan/Feb		ideal under trees
ft		E	large dark green	large white Nov/Feb		
in		E		lavender blue, scented Jan/Feb		poor soils for maximum flowering
in		E	succulent, tight rosettes	purplish to pale yellow June/Aug		many varieties ideal for rockeries and walls

Index

Index

Index

Index

CANCELLED
STIRLING
DISTRICT
LIBRARY